Gates of Shabbat
שערי שבת

Gates of Shabbat

שַׁעֲרֵי שַׁבָּת

A Guide for Observing Shabbat

Mark Dov Shapiro

Illustrated by Neil Waldman

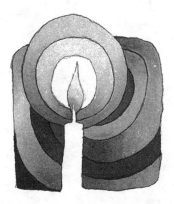

Central Conference of American Rabbis
New York, New York

An audiotape for the Shabbat music in this book is available for purchase from Transcontinental Music Publications, Inc., 838 Fifth Avenue, New York, NY 10021. Sheet music with piano arrangements and/or guitar chording for most of the music is also available from Transcontinental.

The CCAR Press
Central Conference of American Rabbis
192 Lexington Avenue, New York, NY 10016

Library of Congress Cataloging-in-Publication Data

Shapiro, Mark Dov. 1950–
  Sha-a-rei Shabbat = Gates of Shabbat : a guide for observing
Shabbat / Mark Dov Shapiro : illustrated by Neil Waldman.
      p. cm.
  Includes bibliographical references and index.
  ISBN 0-88123-010-3 : $9.95
  1. Sabbath. 2. Reform Judaism—Customs and practices.
3. Sabbath—Liturgy—Texts. 4. Reform Judaism—Liturgy—Texts.
I. Central Conference of American Rabbis. II. Title. III. Title: Gates
of Shabbat. Iv. Title: Shaarei Shabbat.
BM685.S424 1991
296.4'1—dc20   90-48395
                                                  CIP

Designed by Barry Nostradamus Sher. Composed at
Nostradamus Advertising using Xerox Ventura Publisher 2.0 with
Professional Extension. English text set in Palatino, designed by
Hermann Zapf and digitized by Adobe Systems. Hebrew text set
in Lev Yaakov, designed and digitized by Lawrence Kushner.
Publisher's Type Foundry was used to re-map Lev Yaakov and
create specialized characters. Music set by Jim Legg, using Finale.

Contents

A Note on Transliteration

The system employed in this book is, with minor deviations, the "Proposed Standard Romanization of Hebrew" prepared for the American National Standards Institute, and used in all liturgy published by the Central Conference of American Rabbis.

Vowels and Consonants for Special Notice

a	as in 'papa' (short) or 'father' (long)
e	as in 'get' or 'the' (sheva)
eh	as in 'get' (used only at the end of a word)
i	as in 'bit' (short) or 'machine' (long)
o	as in 'often'
u	as in 'pull' (short) or 'rule' (long)
ai	as in 'aisle'
oi	as in 'boil'
ei	as in 'veil'
g	as in 'get' (hard)
ch	as in Scottish 'loch' or German 'ach'

Foreword

A generation ago Reform Judaism entered into a new age of religious discipline. With the publication of *A Shabbat Manual* by Rabbi W. Gunther Plaut, an authoritative guide for Sabbath observance was welcomed into the lives of Reform Jews. As a consequence of that first guidebook for Reform Jewish observance, mitzvot were given new vitality and rituals were endowed with added significance.

Following the successful publication of *A Shabbat Manual*, it became clear that there was a need for additional guides to festival and life cycle rituals. Thus the Central Conference of American Rabbis published *Shaarei Mitzvah/Gates of Mitzvah* and *Shaarei Mo-eid/Gates of the Seasons*, works that encouraged Reform Jews to live by the mitzvot.

An undergirding principle of Reform Judaism holds that each generation is obliged to define for itself the way it will interpret and act out the mitzvot. It was that sense of generational need that mandated the publication of this new manual for Sabbath observance, *Shaarei Shabbat/Gates of Shabbat*.

So much has happened since the first mitzvah manual was produced. Wholly new liturgies have been published by the Central Conference of American Rabbis for synagogue, home, and rabbinic use. Recently established commissions have studied and worked in the areas of religious living and synagogue music to foster an appreciation of traditional expressions of Judaism. At the same time, of course, no area of Jewish life is to be excluded from the fundamental ideal that Reform Judaism is always in process. So it is right that our guides for Jewish living should be reexamined and recast in keeping with our current self-definition.

Thus Shabbat observance for the contemporary Jew is defined anew in this newly created volume. To his credit, Rabbi Mark Shapiro has followed certain of the directions contained in the earlier Shabbat guidebook, but diverged from these directions to allow a new generation to explore the dimensions of Shabbat in our time. His is an invaluable contribution to the liturgical and practical ways in which Reform Jewish living can be enhanced in this new era. This informative and inspirational volume, this *Shaarei Shabbat*, is but the latest testimony to the Reform Jewish principle of ongoing redefinition.

H. Leonard Poller, Chair,
C.C.A.R. Liturgy Committee

Preface

This book emerged out of a dialogue about Shabbat and Jewish observance that I have been privileged to conduct with many dedicated Reform Jews over the last several years.

A group of congregants from my previous congregation were instrumental in setting the tone for the book. Many colleagues and good friends then offered their own insights. These included the members of the Liturgy and Religious Practices Committees of the Central Conference of American Rabbis and, in particular, Rabbis H. Leonard Poller, Peter Knobel, Stephen Pearce, and Robert Loewy who formed a dedicated and wonderfully perceptive Editorial Committee. Rabbi Elliot Stevens was a tremendous resource as friend and expert at every stage of development. Daniel Schechter, Barry Sher of Nostradamus Advertising, Louise Stern, Rabbis Morrison David Bial, Steven Bob, Norman M. Cohen, Gary Bretton-Granatoor, David Cahn-Lipman, Steven Chatinover, Bruce Ehrman, Lawrence Englander, Daniel H. Freelander, Elyse Goldstein, Walter Jacob, Robert Klensin, Mark Levin, Robert Levine, Michael Mayersohn, David Fox Sandmel, Joshua Segal, Charles Sherman, Elliot Strom, and my teacher, W. Gunther Plaut, all offered support that was enduring and crucial as the manuscript developed.

The entire project would not have reached its conclusion, however, without the inspiration of my wife, Marsha. She, along with Jordan and Daniel, give each week and each Shabbat the joy that makes everything else possible.

Rabbi Mark Dov Shapiro
Sinai Temple
Springfield, Massachusetts

Sivan 5751
June 1991

The Possibilities of Shabbat

An artist cannot be continually wielding the brush. The artist must stop painting at times to freshen the vision of the object, the meaning of which is to be expressed on canvas. Living is also an art. The Shabbat represents those moments when we pause in our brushwork to renew our vision of the object. Having done so, we take ourselves to our painting with clarified vision and renewed energy.

Mordecai M. Kaplan

Invitation

This is a book about the art of living as it expresses itself through Shabbat.

If you are unsure about the significance of Shabbat and are searching for a guidebook to lead you into the experience, this book is for you. If you are already committed to the Shabbat "pause" in your life and want to deepen your observance, this book is also for you.

Above all else, the premise here is that Jewish living involves learning and discovery. You will, therefore, find a wide variety of opportunities for Shabbat experimentation and growth in these pages. Even though you may not "do it all" at the outset, the key to Shabbat lies in at least beginning.

Hence, the invitation of this book. Read and learn; experience what you can of Shabbat. Open *Shaarei Shabbat/Gates of Shabbat* and discover the spirit of a day that can mean so much in your life as a Jew.

What Can Shabbat Mean?

We begin with a story:

> Looking out the window on a weekday morning, the Chasidic teacher, Nachman of Bratzlav, noticed his disciple, Chaim, rushing along the street.

> Reb Nachman opened the window and invited Chaim to come inside. Chaim entered the home and Nachman said to him, "Chaim, have you seen the sky this morning?" "No, Rebbe," answered Chaim. "Have you seen the street this morning?" "Yes, Rebbe." "Tell me, please, Chaim, what did you see in the street?" "I saw people, carts, and merchandise. I saw merchants and peasants all coming and going, selling and buying."

"Chaim," said Nachman, "in 50 years, in 100 years, on that very street there will be a market. Other vehicles will then bring merchants and merchandise to the street. But I won't be here then and neither will you. So, I ask you, Chaim, *what's the good of your rushing if you don't even have time to look at the sky?*

The world of today, like the world of the eighteenth century Rebbe, is busy and often frantic. Schedules overwhelm us and in many cases seem to rule us, so that "the sky" and an appreciation of life's broader purpose pass us by daily. Our lives are often consumed in activity without any feeling for the joy of the moment.

Shabbat is the vehicle by which Judaism addresses this dilemma. It is a time for stepping back from the busyness of life to gain perspective on the meaning of life.

Shabbat is an opportunity for "time out" from the pressures of the work week. It allows us to make time for those people and experiences that matter to us most.

To give the day what Judaism calls a sense of *kedusha* or holiness, we re-focus our activities. That may simply mean changing pace for dinner on Friday evening. However, as this book will suggest, Shabbat offers many other ways for stepping outside the realm of our usual lifestyle.

The Book of Exodus (31:16–17) offers a model for Shabbat observance with a twofold description of what God did after creating the world. Exodus tells us that on the first Shabbat, "God rested and was refreshed."

In our terms, God's "rest" signifies that Shabbat involves stopping weekday activities in order to leave behind our weekday mind-set. At the same time, Shabbat rest is meant to be more than mere relaxation. It is a means to the end of "refreshing" ourselves.

As Rabbi Mordecai M. Kaplan teaches, "The Shabbat represents those moments when we pause in our brushwork to renew our vision." We make the day an occasion for freeing ourselves from weekday restraints in order to become the fully human persons we want to be.

And yet Shabbat is more than a private time for introspection. Shabbat is more than a pleasant day away from the office.

Shabbat is an intrinsically Jewish experience, which means that the rest and refreshment of Shabbat take on added dimension because they are structured in a Jewish fashion. *Shabbat allows us to deal with the turmoil of contemporary life in the context of Judaism.*

In our society, where the pace of life is hectic and where the moral ground shifts so rapidly, Shabbat is important because it can anchor us weekly in ceremonies and values sanctified by centuries of Jewish life.

Shabbat reminds us that Jews need never stand alone. We can always draw on our roots in the Jewish experience, our connections to other Jews, our relationship to Torah, and the berit/covenant with God.

A Note on Using This Guide

Shaarei Shabbat tries to make the various aspects of Shabbat as accessible as possible. If you want to begin immediately, turn to the pages containing the prayers for observing Shabbat at home. You will find there the various blessings and directions you need in order to start bringing Shabbat into your life.

If you are looking for greater understanding, consult the background material presented throughout the guide in a question-and-answer format. You should also read the sections of the text that present ideas on the role of the synagogue and the challenge of developing a contemporary definition for "rest" on the seventh day.

The section "Readings and Meditations" offers a combination of prose and poetry that is both informative and inspirational. The material in this section can be used to enhance the home services for Shabbat.

The final section of the guide discusses the directions you can follow in continuing to refine your commitment to Shabbat. Under the heading, "The Mitzvot of Shabbat," you will find a summary of the ways in which a Reform Jew can approach Shabbat. You will also find a concluding invitation to carry on with the process of Jewish learning and growth that gives life to this volume.

As you begin your journey through the "gates of Shabbat," you may also want to bear in mind the words of a classic Shabbat prayer—"Those who keep Shabbat and call it a joy shall delight in God's rule." The prayer highlights the hope that Shabbat will become a source of joy in your life. Your celebration of this day can offer you a sense of satisfaction and fulfillment that is the unique gift of Jewish tradition.

Questions and Answers

Shabbat sounds wonderful, almost too good to be true. What if it doesn't mean as much to me as it does to some other Jews?

It is quite possible that Shabbat is not as high a priority in your life as it is in the lives of some Jews. Your Shabbat may not even resemble the ideal Shabbat described in many parts of this book. That does not matter at this point. What matters is that you begin to learn. Many options for interpreting and observing Shabbat are offered in these pages so that different people in varying circumstances can all find something of significance. The meaning of Shabbat is not a given. It grows as you begin to encounter Shabbat from wherever you find yourself now as a Jew.

Where do I begin if I'm a novice?

Begin simply. Look over the possibilities described in this book and choose one or two ways to observe Shabbat. Starting with candlelighting on Friday night is one of the easiest ways to enter Shabbat. Whatever you choose, remember you don't need to restructure your entire lifestyle in one weekend! Just give yourself some time to experience Shabbat and the day will begin to take shape.

Even at that, don't be surprised if your "new" Shabbat also changes with time. You should continue to grow as a Jew so that Shabbat takes on greater meaning with the passing years. The process of "making" Shabbat is truly lifelong.

Should all the prayers be recited in Hebrew?

It is not necessary to read Hebrew in order to begin your observance of Shabbat. The blessings in this book are translated so that anyone can have access to them. Hopefully, your enriched experience at home and in the synagogue will at some point lead to your learning to read and understand Hebrew if you cannot yet do so.

Everyone in our home works. How can we find the time to prepare for Shabbat and make the day different?

If your days are already so full that finding time for any new activity, let alone Shabbat, seems unrealistic, you will probably not find time for Shabbat by simply hoping some "open" moments will appear on the weekend calendar. The open moments will only appear if you decide in advance that *you want to make them appear*. In other words, you will need to make time for the time to observe Shabbat.

That might involve starting to think about Shabbat as early as Monday. Early in the week you may need to choose a Friday evening menu or plan a special activity suitable for Shabbat day.

When Friday evening actually arrives, try an experiment to help yourself get started. For a set period of four weeks commit yourself to a particular ritual like the Friday evening Kiddush. Promise yourself to do the Kiddush under almost all circumstances.

That discipline might be just what you need to begin to make the Kiddush a habit. After four weeks, even if you do once again become "too busy" for Kiddush, you may discover that your familiarity with the Kiddush has made it into something you miss. You will find yourself making time for the Kiddush because it has become a natural part of your life.

By the way, the welcoming of Shabbat from candles to challah does not take much time. It can take as little as five minutes to say the blessings, or somewhat more time if you complement the blessings with singing and the other possibilities discussed below.

I'm a single person. How can I have Shabbat?

You can have Shabbat by not allowing yourself to think about Shabbat or Judaism as solely a family affair. The Shabbat message about sanctifying time and renewing our relationship with prayer and Jewish study is very much directed to individual, adult Jews.

Despite that, those parts of Shabbat that do focus on the home, especially Friday evening's dinner, can be difficult for the single person. Even though the blessings can all be done by an individual of either sex,[1] many people will be more comfortable sharing dinner with others. For that reason it makes sense to plan ahead and arrange to spend Friday evening with friends or family. The essence of Shabbat, however, is still very much yours as a single, Jewish adult.

My spouse is not Jewish. How do we observe Shabbat?

If your spouse is willing to join you in exploring Shabbat, the two of you ought to begin together. Even though a non-Jew might not feel comfortable reciting blessings with such phrases as "who has commanded *us*," Shabbat allows so many possibilities for observance and enjoyment that it can act as a powerful mechanism for giving your home a Jewish ambience.

Observing Shabbat

Welcoming Shabbat

Come, my beloved. Let us go out to meet the bride. Let us greet Shabbat.
From the sixteenth century song, *Lecha Dodi*

Jewish tradition compares the arrival of Shabbat to the arrival of an important guest. In the sixteenth century, the Jewish mystics of Safed in the land of Israel took this imagery so seriously that on Friday afternoons they would dress in white as if they were going to a wedding. As the sun set and Shabbat began, they would go to the outskirts of their town to "welcome the Sabbath bride."

To this day Shabbat is referred to as both a bride and a queen. The understanding is that in order to greet Shabbat properly, special preparations must be made.

Preparations

According to the rabbis,[2] the commandment to prepare for Shabbat is implied in the Ten Commandments as they appear in the Book of Exodus (20:8)—"Remember Shabbat and keep it holy." How does one "remember" Shabbat? The answer is that one remembers Shabbat by keeping it in mind and anticipating it as the days of the week go by.

The Talmud[3] also relates that everyone in the community became involved in preparing for Shabbat. Even the leading rabbis stopped their weekday activities early enough on Friday to participate in preparing meals, gathering wood, and getting out proper dishes for Shabbat.

In our day, too, stopping early and preparing for Shabbat can be the first steps in observing Shabbat. This can involve shopping for appropriate Shabbat food earlier in the week, baking or buying challah, and preparing the special meal often associated with Friday evening. (See page 30 for more details on the Shabbat meal.)

At the same time, preparing for Shabbat need not only mean logging hours in the kitchen. In fact, in this era of dual-career families a complicated dinner menu may prove to be an obstacle to Shabbat rather than an incentive. Because of that, some people may concentrate their efforts on welcoming Shabbat in areas other than cooking. Consider these possibilities for enhancing the beginning of your Shabbat:

Purchase flowers to beautify your table for Shabbat

If children are involved, let them accompany you and help choose the flowers.

Use different dishes for the Friday evening meal

When it comes to the Kiddush over the wine, try to use cups that are specifically set aside for that purpose. Even though standard wineglasses and weekday dishes will suffice, special tableware is more appropriate, because it draws on the Jewish custom of *hidur mitzvah*—the belief that the spirit of any celebration is enhanced when it is carried out as beautifully as possible. On the same principle, you can make your meal special by using attractive linens or moving the meal to the dining room.

**Dress differently for the Friday evening meal,
if not all of Shabbat day**

The Talmud[4] recommends this practice. A clean shirt or blouse (white is a traditional Shabbat color) for everyone at dinner might set the tone.

**If children are present, let them help as
much as they can in preparing**

They might set the table or create decorations for Shabbat.

Open your home to guests

Ideally, no one should have to observe Shabbat alone. Judaism even understands the act of hachnasat orchim/hospitality as a mitzvah/commandment, which means that by sharing Shabbat with someone outside your family, you are giving extra Jewish significance to the seventh day.

Be there

For those who are just beginning to approach Shabbat, being home for dinner may constitute *the* major change of pace. Leaving work in time to be present when the rest of the family eats may mean thinking about Friday's schedule one day or possibly several days in advance. It may mean breaking a series of old work habits in order to make space in your life for a new Jewish commitment.

Finally, when you think about Shabbat, it is important to remember that Shabbat extends beyond Friday evening's meal. Preparing for Shabbat can, therefore, involve much more than preparing for Kabbalat Shabbat (the welcoming of Shabbat around the dinner table). It can involve making room in your schedule for the many aspects of Shabbat that extend through Friday night and into Saturday.

Tzedakah/Charity

It is customary to make charitable donations just before Shabbat arrives. This can be done at your table with everyone in the household putting some change in a suitable collection box (*pushke*). Every few weeks you can then have a discussion as to where the tzedakah money collected ought to go.

In some households family members save the requests for donations that they receive in the mail. When the family discusses how to distribute its tzedakah, these requests are brought to the table so that the entire family can decide which organizations ought to receive support.

Further Options

You may add to your Shabbat experience by trying some of the following. They can be done at any point in the Shabbat rituals.

A special prayer or reading

One or more of those present can write their own Shabbat thought or prayer. It can be as simple as a brief wish for those around the table that evening. Others can participate at the table by reading a poem or a relevant article. Suitable readings can be found later in this book (see "Readings and Meditations," page 73) as well as in *Gates of Prayer* and *Gates of the House*.

Something good

Each person (preschooler as well as grandparents) completes this phrase as you go around the table: "Something good happened to me this week. It was…."

Proud time

Looking back on the previous week, each person completes this phrase: "I'm proud that I…."

The past week

Without using either of the above two discussion starters, you might simply invite those at your table to reflect on some of the events of the past week.

Erev Shabbat / Friday Evening
The Home Service

Erev Shabbat / Friday Evening
The Home Service

The Sabbath is a queen whose coming changes the humblest home into a palace.

Talmud *Shabbat* 119a

The holy Shabbat is the greatest gift given us by the Holy One. So we should rejoice in the coming of Shabbat. If the expectation of a special guest would cause us to prepare with great care, how much more so should we act when the guest is the Shabbat Bride. Fresh coverings should be set aside for Friday evening. Something special should even be eaten on Shabbat. Everyone, even someone with servants, must do something himself to honor Shabbat whether it be helping prepare the meal, cleaning the house, or purchasing flowers to adorn the Shabbat table.

Joseph Caro, *Shulchan Aruch*,
Sixteenth century

Hadlakat Neirot
Candlelighting

Introduction
(You may read one of the following.)

In kindling Sabbath light,
we preserve life's sanctity.
With every holy light we kindle,
the world is brightened to a higher harmony.

*(When children are present,
more than one reader might share this passage.)*

Shabbat can be different from any other day.
Shabbat can be many things.

> *Shabbat can be the beauty of the candles
> as we light them at our table.*

Shabbat can be singing the Kiddush and tasting sweet wine.

> *Shabbat can be biting into the soft, golden challah.*

Shabbat can be a blessing for the family.

> *Shabbat can be saying thank you, God, for our whole family.*

The Blessing

Light the candles and then recite the blessing.

♪ See page 109

Ba-ruch a-ta, A-do-nai	בָּרוּךְ אַתָּה, יְיָ
E-lo-hei-nu, me-lech ha-o-lam,	אֱלֹהֵינוּ, מֶלֶךְ הָעוֹלָם,
a-sher ki-de-sha-nu be-mits-vo-tav,	אֲשֶׁר קִדְּשָׁנוּ בְּמִצְוֹתָיו,
ve-tsi-va-nu le-had-lik	וְצִוָּנוּ לְהַדְלִיק
neir shel Sha-bat.	נֵר שֶׁל שַׁבָּת.

We praise You, Adonai our God, Ruler of the universe, who has made us holy with commandments and commanded us to kindle the lights of Shabbat.

(The service continues on page 18.)

What is the origin of the Shabbat candles?

The practice of kindling lights at the beginning of Shabbat is first mentioned in post-biblical literature. By the time of its completion at the end of the second century C.E., the Mishnah assumes that Shabbat begins with the kindling of lights, and it goes into detail about the proper kind of wicks to be used for the oil lamps of that time.[5]

In later times, when the oil lamp was replaced by candles, it became customary to have a minimum of two lights for Shabbat. These two candles correspond to the two different words (zachor/remember and shamor/observe) that begin the Shabbat commandment in the two versions of the Ten Commandments (Exodus 20:8 and Deuteronomy 5:12).

Who lights the candles?

The Jewish codes of law (Maimonides, *Mishneh Torah*, twelfth century and Joseph Caro, *Shulchan Aruch*, sixteenth century) obligate both men and women to light Shabbat candles. Thus if there are no women present in the home or a male is travelling alone, he is responsible for lighting the Shabbat candles.

Despite this ruling of equal obligation for the candles, the lighting of the candles became a mitzvah more closely associated with women. This probably happened because of the traditional Shabbat schedule according to which men would be at the synagogue welcoming Shabbat while women were in the home prior to sunset when the time for candlelighting arrived.

How are the candles lit?

Usually when you perform a mitzvah requiring a blessing, you recite the blessing and then perform the act. For example, with the Kiddush, the blessing is recited first and then the wine is drunk. However, kindling the Shabbat candles follows a different procedure. Since the blessing marks the formal beginning of Shabbat, and since according to the traditional definition of work lighting a fire on Shabbat is prohibited, you first light the candles (technically before Shabbat) and then recite the blessing (thereby beginning Shabbat).

In many homes it is customary for those who light the candles to cover their eyes or use their hands to block the candles from view while saying the blessing. Custom has it that at this moment, when the candles are not seen, it is as if the candles had not been lit. When the blessing is complete and Shabbat has begun, the candles are then revealed as lit.

When are the candles lit?

The lighting of candles marks the formal beginning of Shabbat. Most Reform Jews therefore light their candles whenever they begin their Shabbat meal. Others follow the custom of linking the beginning of Shabbat to the time of sunset on Friday. In this case Jewish calendars, which are printed annually, specify the time for candlelighting each week. The time is set eighteen minutes before sunset in order to be sure that the candles are not lit any later than sunset.

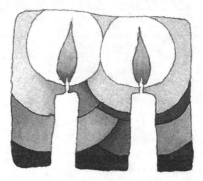

Shalom Aleichem
A Song of Peace

See page 110

(You may sing the following song.)

Sha-lom a-lei-chem, mal-a-chei
ha-sha-reit, mal-a-chei El-yon,
mi-me-lech ma-le-chei ha-me-la-chim,
ha-ka-dosh ba-ruch Hu.

שָׁלוֹם עֲלֵיכֶם, מַלְאֲכֵי
הַשָּׁרֵת, מַלְאֲכֵי עֶלְיוֹן,
מִמֶּלֶךְ מַלְכֵי הַמְּלָכִים,
הַקָּדוֹשׁ בָּרוּךְ הוּא.

Bo-a-chem le-sha-lom, mal-a-chei
ha-sha-lom, mal-a-chei El-yon,
mi-me-lech ma-le-chei ha-me-la-chim,
ha-ka-dosh ba-ruch Hu.

בּוֹאֲכֶם לְשָׁלוֹם, מַלְאֲכֵי
הַשָּׁלוֹם, מַלְאֲכֵי עֶלְיוֹן,
מִמֶּלֶךְ מַלְכֵי הַמְּלָכִים,
הַקָּדוֹשׁ בָּרוּךְ הוּא.

Ba-re-chu-ni le-sha-lom, mal-a-chei
ha-sha-lom, mal-a-chei El-yon,
mi-me-lech ma-le-chei ha-me-la-chim,
ha-ka-dosh ba-ruch Hu.

בָּרְכוּנִי לְשָׁלוֹם, מַלְאֲכֵי
הַשָּׁלוֹם, מַלְאֲכֵי עֶלְיוֹן,
מִמֶּלֶךְ מַלְכֵי הַמְּלָכִים,
הַקָּדוֹשׁ בָּרוּךְ הוּא.

Tsei-te-chem le-sha-lom, mal-a-chei
ha-sha-lom, mal-a-chei El-yon,
mi-me-lech ma-le-chei ha-me-la-chim,
ha-ka-dosh ba-ruch Hu.

צֵאתְכֶם לְשָׁלוֹם, מַלְאֲכֵי
הַשָּׁלוֹם, מַלְאֲכֵי עֶלְיוֹן,
מִמֶּלֶךְ מַלְכֵי הַמְּלָכִים,
הַקָּדוֹשׁ בָּרוּךְ הוּא.

Peace be to you, O ministering angels, messengers of the Most
High, the supreme Ruler of rulers, the Holy One of blessing.
Enter in peace, O messengers of peace, messengers of the Most
High, the supreme Ruler of rulers, the Holy One of blessing.
Bless me with peace, O messengers of peace, messengers of the
Most High, the supreme Ruler of rulers, the Holy One of
blessing.
Depart in peace, O messengers of peace, messengers of the Most
High, the supreme Ruler of rulers, the Holy One of blessing.

(The service continues on page 20.)

What is the connection between this song and the Friday evening home service?

"Shalom Aleichem," which dates from the seventeenth century, became a customary home song because of its connection with the talmudic legend that two angels accompany a Jew on the way home from synagogue on Friday evening. If the home has been prepared to honor Shabbat, the good angel says, "So may it be next Shabbat," and the evil angel reluctantly says, "Amen." If the home is not ready for Shabbat, the evil angel can say, "So may it be next Shabbat," and the good angel must respond, "Amen."[6]

Why is music used to welcome Shabbat?

The singing and chanting of songs and blessings have become a customary part of Shabbat because Jewish tradition has always associated Shabbat with oneg/joy. Although music is not necessary around your table (you can recite the blessings as opposed to chanting them), you certainly ought to try singing on Shabbat. With a bit of practice, your chanting of the blessings and singing of Shalom Aleichem or other songs can become an integral part of your observance.

Birkat Hamishpacha
Family Blessing

Place your hands on your child's head or shoulders or hold your child's hands and recite the following blessings.

(You can also supplement the prayers written here with your own words or a silent prayer.)

For a boy:

Ye-sim-cha E-lo-him ke-ef-ra-yim

ve-chi-me-na-sheh.

יְשִׂמְךָ אֱלֹהִים כְּאֶפְרַיִם וְכִמְנַשֶּׁה.

May God inspire you to live in the tradition of Ephraim and Manasseh, who carried forward the life of our people.

For a girl:

Ye-si-meich E-lo-him

ke-sa-ra, riv-ka, ra-cheil, ve-lei-a.

יְשִׂמֵךְ אֱלֹהִים כְּשָׂרָה, רִבְקָה, רָחֵל, וְלֵאָה.

May God inspire you to live in the tradition of Sarah and Rebekah, Rachel and Leah, who carried forward the life of our people.

After the separate prayers for boys or girls, continue for both:

Ye-va-re-che-cha A-do-nai

ve-yish-me-re-cha.

Ya-eir A-do-nai pa-nav

ei-le-cha vi-chu-ne-ka.

Yi-sa A-do-nai pa-nav ei-le-cha

ve-ya-seim le-cha sha-lom.

יְבָרֶכְךָ יְיָ וְיִשְׁמְרֶךָ. יָאֵר יְיָ פָּנָיו אֵלֶיךָ וִיחֻנֶּךָּ. יִשָּׂא יְיָ פָּנָיו אֵלֶיךָ וְיָשֵׂם לְךָ שָׁלוֹם.

May God bless you and guard you. May the light of God shine upon you, and may God be gracious to you. May the presence of God be with you and give you peace.

(The service continues on page 22.)

Where does the custom of blessing children originate?

The Torah presents several instances of children being blessed. For example, Isaac blesses his sons, Jacob and Esau, and Jacob blesses his twelve sons (Genesis 27, 49). Jacob also blesses his grandsons Ephraim and Manasseh, and the words he uses in Genesis 48:20 provide the customary wording of the blessing used for sons at the Shabbat table.

The blessing for girls incorporates the names of the matriarchs whose actions in the Book of Genesis helped shape the earliest experiences of our people.

What are the component parts of the Shabbat evening blessing?

1. The blessing begins with separate prayers for boys and girls.
2. The threefold "priestly blessing" follows. It is taken from the Book of Numbers (6:24–26).

How do I do the blessing? How will my children feel about it?

Since the blessing does involve communicating with your child in what is probably not your usual style, you and your child may feel strange when you first do it. The formal nature of the recitation may almost obscure the wonderful intimacy of the moment.

Because of that you may at first choose to abbreviate the experience by doing only part 1 or part 2 of the blessing. You might also have all the adults and children gathered around the table hold hands so as not to focus solely on the children during the blessing.

However you proceed, remember that the family blessing adds something beautiful to your family's experience of Shabbat.

Are there ways to extend the idea of blessing beyond the children to include adults?

There most certainly are ways to share blessings among adults. A husband can recite verses from chapter 31 of the Book of Proverbs referring to his wife as "a woman of valor" (see page 74). A wife can recite from Psalm 112 for her husband (see page 74). A family prayer can also be read for all those at the table (see page 82).

Finally, rather than using a prewritten text, people at the table can consider sharing some of their own reflections on the week gone and the week yet to come.

Kiddush
Sanctifying Shabbat

Introduction

(You may read one of the following.)

The seventh day is consecrated to God. With wine, our symbol of joy, we celebrate this day and its holiness. We give thanks for all our blessings, for life and health, for work and rest, for home and love and friendship. On Shabbat, eternal sign of creation, we remember that we are created in the divine image. We therefore raise the cup in thanksgiving.

(When children are present, more than one reader might share this passage.)

When God made the world, God made it full of light:
the sun to shine by day, the moon and stars by night.

> *And God said, "Let the earth bring forth plants and trees*
> *of every kind."*

God made the world full of living things,
walking and flying, hopping and swimming.

> *And the Torah tells us God saw that the world was good.*

And God made man and woman and gave them
minds and hearts and hands,
to think and to feel, to work and to play.

> *And God saw everything in the world, and, behold,*
> *it was very good.*

So there was morning and evening, and after six days of creation,
heaven and earth, the entire world, was made.

> *Only one thing more remained to be created.*
> *As a ruler needs a crown, the world needed its own crown.*
> *So God made the seventh day into Shabbat*
> *and called it a crown for the world.*

Shabbat…A time to look at our world and enjoy its beauty. A day for thanking God for health and love, for family and for friends.

> *We thank God now for our blessings by singing the Kiddush.*

When we taste the sweetness of the grapes, we say:
Thank You, God, for all that is sweet in our lives.

The Concluding Day of Creation

(As a reminder of the origin of Shabbat, you can use the following Torah verses to introduce the Kiddush. The verses can be said in Hebrew or English.)

Va-ye-hi e-rev, va-ye-hi vo-ker,	וַיְהִי עֶרֶב, וַיְהִי בֹקֶר,
yom ha-shi-shi.	יוֹם הַשִּׁשִּׁי.
Va-ye-chu-lu	וַיְכֻלּוּ
ha-sha-ma-yim ve-ha-a-rets	הַשָּׁמַיִם וְהָאָרֶץ
ve-chol tse-va-am,	וְכָל־צְבָאָם,
va-ye-chal E-lo-him	וַיְכַל אֱלֹהִים
ba-yom ha-she-vi-i	בַּיּוֹם הַשְּׁבִיעִי
me-lach-to a-sher a-sa;	מְלַאכְתּוֹ אֲשֶׁר עָשָׂה;
va-yish-bot ba-yom ha-she-vi-i	וַיִּשְׁבֹּת בַּיּוֹם הַשְּׁבִיעִי
mi-kol me-lach-to a-sher a-sa.	מִכָּל־מְלַאכְתּוֹ אֲשֶׁר עָשָׂה.
Va-ye-va-rech E-lo-him	וַיְבָרֶךְ אֱלֹהִים
et yom ha-she-vi-i	אֶת־יוֹם הַשְּׁבִיעִי
va-ye-ka-deish o-to,	וַיְקַדֵּשׁ אֹתוֹ,
ki vo sha-vat mi-kol me-lach-to	כִּי בוֹ שָׁבַת מִכָּל־מְלַאכְתּוֹ
a-sher ba-ra E-lo-him la-a-sot.	אֲשֶׁר־בָּרָא אֱלֹהִים לַעֲשׂוֹת.

And there was evening and there was morning, the sixth day. The heaven and the earth were finished and all their array. And on the seventh day God finished the work which God had been doing, and God ceased on the seventh day from all the work which had been done. And God blessed the seventh day and declared it holy, because on it God ceased from all the work of creation which had been done.

(Genesis 1:31, 2:1–3)

Blessing over the Wine

Raise the Kiddush cups filled with wine or grape juice.
(The Kiddush can be said or sung with those present either standing or sitting.)

♪ See page 111

Ba-ruch a-ta, A-do-nai	בָּרוּךְ אַתָּה, יְיָ
E-lo-hei-nu, me-lech ha-o-lam,	אֱלֹהֵינוּ, מֶלֶךְ הָעוֹלָם,
bo-rei pe-ri ha-ga-fen.	בּוֹרֵא פְּרִי הַגָּפֶן.

We praise You, Adonai, our God, Ruler of the universe, Creator of the fruit of the vine.

Sanctifying
Shabbat

Ba-ruch a-ta, A-do-nai	בָּרוּךְ אַתָּה, יְיָ
E-lo-hei-nu, me-lech ha-o-lam,	אֱלֹהֵינוּ, מֶלֶךְ הָעוֹלָם,
a-sher ki-de-sha-nu be-mits-vo-tav	אֲשֶׁר קִדְּשָׁנוּ בְּמִצְוֹתָיו
ve-ra-tsa va-nu,	וְרָצָה בָנוּ,
ve-sha-bat kod-sho	וְשַׁבַּת קָדְשׁוֹ
be-a-ha-va u-ve-ra-tson	בְּאַהֲבָה וּבְרָצוֹן
hin-chi-la-nu, zi-ka-ron	הִנְחִילָנוּ, זִכָּרוֹן
le-ma-a-sei ve-rei-shit.	לְמַעֲשֵׂה בְרֵאשִׁית.
Ki hu yom te-chi-la,	כִּי הוּא יוֹם תְּחִלָּה
le-mik-ra-ei ko-desh,	לְמִקְרָאֵי קֹדֶשׁ,
zei-cher li-tsi-at Mits-ra-yim.	זֵכֶר לִיצִיאַת מִצְרָיִם.
Ki va-nu va-char-ta,	כִּי־בָנוּ בָחַרְתָּ,
ve-o-ta-nu ki-dash-ta	וְאוֹתָנוּ קִדַּשְׁתָּ
mi-kol ha-a-mim,	מִכָּל־הָעַמִּים,
ve-sha-bat kod-she-cha	וְשַׁבַּת קָדְשְׁךָ
be-a-ha-va u-ve-ra-tson	בְּאַהֲבָה וּבְרָצוֹן
hin-chal-ta-nu.	הִנְחַלְתָּנוּ:
Ba-ruch a-ta, A-do-nai,	בָּרוּךְ אַתָּה, יְיָ,
me-ka-deish ha-sha-bat.	מְקַדֵּשׁ הַשַּׁבָּת.

We praise You, Adonai our God, Ruler of the universe who hallows us with mitzvot and favors us with the holy Shabbat, lovingly and graciously bestowed upon us, a memorial of the act of creation, first of the holy assemblies, a remembrance of the going forth from Egypt.

You have chosen us and hallowed us from among all peoples, by lovingly and graciously bestowing upon us Your holy Sabbath. We praise You, O God, who sanctifies Shabbat.

Drink the wine.
(The service continues on page 27.)

What does "Kiddush" mean?

Kiddush is the Hebrew word for "sanctification." It comes from the same Hebrew root as the word *kadosh*, which means "holy" or "set apart."

What is the structure of the Kiddush?

The Friday evening Kiddush consists of:

1. The one line blessing over the wine (...*borei peri hagafen*/Creator of the fruit of the vine).

2. The blessing sanctifying the day of Shabbat. (This is the full Hebrew paragraph on page 24, concluding with the words of blessing: *Baruch ata, Adonai, mekadeish hashabat* / We praise You, O God, who sanctifies Shabbat.)

What is the purpose of the Kiddush?

The Kiddush is the prayer with which we sanctify Shabbat. The rabbis reasoned that there was an obligation to sanctify Shabbat as a result of their reading of the Shabbat commandment in the Book of Exodus (20:8). Where that text says "Remember the Sabbath day to keep it holy," the rabbis determined that making Shabbat holy meant sanctifying it with a blessing.[7] The two-part Kiddush on Friday night is that blessing.

How does wine become involved in the Kiddush?

Because Shabbat is associated with joy ("You shall call the Sabbath a *joy*," Isaiah 58:13) and because wine is also understood in Jewish tradition to be a symbol of joy ("Wine makes *glad* the human heart," Psalms 104:15), the rabbis declared that Shabbat should be sanctified using wine.[8] It is important to note that the Kiddush is not a prayer in which the wine is sanctified. Rather, it is a prayer in which the wine is used in order to sanctify Shabbat.

If you do not have wine, you may omit the blessing, "...*borei peri hagafen*." Instead, recite the Motsi over bread followed by the Kiddush paragraph which sanctifies Shabbat.

What kind of wine is appropriate for Kiddush?

The kosher wine associated through the ages with Jewish ceremonies was kosher, by definition of the Talmud, if it was produced by Jews alone under rabbinic supervision.[9] Special precautions to ensure that Jews were the only ones involved in producing the wine were taken long ago, because, in the ancient world, wine was used in the libations for idol worship. Lest they unwittingly use wine intended for idolatry, Jews chose to use only their own wine. When idol worship ceased, the rabbinic exclusion of non-Jews from the production of wine persisted as a way of minimizing social contact between Jews and non-Jews.

In our time the rationale for the earlier definition of kosher wine no longer obtains. Some Jews will, therefore, use any wine for Kiddush. In the interest of historic continuity, others choose to use traditional kosher wine. Out of a desire to support Israel, all of whose wines are kosher, some Jews also opt for making Kiddush with Israeli wine.

Should the full text of the Kiddush be said in Hebrew?

Ideally, the Kiddush should be recited in Hebrew. However, English is definitely acceptable. If you possess at least some knowledge of Hebrew, you should be able to do the blessing over the wine in Hebrew while leaving the blessing sanctifying Shabbat in English. As time goes by, you could work towards doing the second blessing in Hebrew by adding a Hebrew sentence or phrase each week.

Why does the Kiddush refer to Shabbat as a reminder of both the Creation of the world *and* the Exodus from Egypt?

The Kiddush contains these two references to the past because the Torah refers to first one and then the other as the historic underpinnings for Shabbat.

In Exodus 20, where the Ten Commandments are proclaimed from Mount Sinai, Jews are called upon to "remember" Shabbat as the day on which God rested after creating the world. Responding to that biblical phrase, the Kiddush mentions creation as a reminder that on Shabbat we follow God's lead and step back from creating and manipulating the world.

In Deuteronomy 5, where Moses repeats the Ten Commandments, the emphasis of the Shabbat commandment is different. There the fourth Commandment calls on Jews to observe Shabbat as a reminder of the Exodus from Egyptian slavery.

According to this understanding of the seventh day, Shabbat calls to mind the experience of liberation. It returns every seven days to help Jews liberate themselves personally from the burdens of the week.

With its focus on liberation, Shabbat ideally achieves even one more purpose. It has the possibility of sensitizing Jews to societal issues of deprivation and injustice. By raising the themes of slavery and freedom, Shabbat can become the gateway to social action during the rest of the week.

What is the significance of the greeting "Lechayim?"

The classic Jewish toast before drinking wine or other beverages is "Lechayim," which means "To life." The toast has talmudic roots insofar as it was the custom during that period to give wine to bereaved persons who were sitting in mourning.[10] When wine was then used in joyous settings, the mood was, of course, very different. To make the distinction clear, the drinking of wine in these settings was accompanied by the hope that it should only be *lechayim* (for life)—for reasons of joy and gladness rather than for grief.

Motsi
Blessing over the Bread

Introduction

(You may read one of the following)

When the world was created,
God made everything a little bit incomplete.
Rather than making bread grow out of the earth,
God made wheat grow so that we might bake it into bread.
Rather than making the earth of bricks,
God made it of clay
    so that we might bake the clay into bricks. Why?
So that we might become partners
    in completing the work of creation.

Before Rabbi Simcha recited the blessing for bread, he would first look at the bare ground. He wanted to be inspired by an appreciation of the contrast between the dust of the earth and the fine bread which it brought forth.

The Blessing

♪ See page 113

The leader places hands on the challah as everyone says the blessing.

Ba-ruch a-ta, A-do-nai

E-lo-hei-nu, me-lech ha-o-lam,

ha-mo-tsi le-chem min ha-a-rets.

בָּרוּךְ אַתָּה, יְיָ

אֱלֹהֵינוּ, מֶלֶךְ הָעוֹלָם,

הַמּוֹצִיא לֶחֶם מִן־הָאָרֶץ.

We praise You, Adonai our God, Ruler of the universe, who brings forth bread from the earth.

Slice or tear the challah and distribute it around the table to be eaten.
Dinner is served.

(Birkat Hamazon, the blessing after the meal, can be found on page 34.)

What is the origin of the term "challah"?

The word "challah" originally referred to the dough offering set aside for the priests during the time of the Jerusalem Temple. After the destruction of the Temple, Jews continued setting aside part of their dough when they baked Shabbat and holiday breads. Eventually, the term "challah" was also applied to these loaves themselves.

Why is a blessing said over the challah?

When we pause to recite the Motsi before a meal begins, our goal is to sensitize ourselves to the fundamental blessings that surround us. We thank God for creating the world in such a way that life can sustain itself.

Why are two loaves used in some homes?

The two loaves represent the double share of manna which, according to the Torah (Exodus 16:22), fell each Friday in order to feed our ancestors on their journey from Egypt to Canaan. Collecting the double portion of manna on Friday meant that the Israelites did not have to collect food when Shabbat arrived.

If you want to have a double share of bread on your table but feel that the two loaves of bread might be wasted in your household, you can use a regular challah with a small roll beside it or simply use two smaller braided challah rolls.

Why is the challah covered until the Motsi in some homes?

Since bread is a basic part of almost every meal, some people keep the challah out of sight in order to highlight the Friday evening ceremonies of candlelighting and Kiddush. Once it is clear that the meal is not an ordinary one but in honor of Shabbat, the challah is uncovered and the Motsi is recited.

Another explanation for this custom is based on the challah's symbolic representation of the manna. The cover over the challah and the plate or platter which is usually placed underneath the challah are said to represent the two layers of dew between which the manna fell, protecting it from the sand of the Sinai desert below and the heat of the sun above.[11]

A popular explanation for children is that the challah is covered in order not to embarrass the bread when the candles and wine are dealt with first. When covering the challah on your table, a napkin can suffice. You can also purchase or even make special challah covers to add to the beauty of your evening.

What is the significance of the handwashing ceremony that precedes the Motsi in some homes?

The custom of washing hands before the Motsi was developed by the talmudic rabbis because of their belief that the family table was as holy as the altar in the Jerusalem Temple where the priests conducted ancient Jewish worship. Just as the priests ritually cleansed their hands before beginning their duties, the rabbis maintained that we ought to wash our hands symbolically before our meals.

Those who wish can participate in this ceremony by going to the sink before the Motsi. Each person grasps a cup or pitcher of water and pours some water from the cup over each hand two or three times. The cup is refilled for the next person until everyone has had a chance. At that point the following blessing is said and the hands are dried.

Ba-ruch a-ta, A-do-nai	בָּרוּךְ אַתָּה, יְיָ
E-lo-hei-nu, me-lech ha-o-lam	אֱלֹהֵינוּ, מֶלֶךְ הָעוֹלָם,
a-sher ki-de-sha-nu be-mits-vo-tav,	אֲשֶׁר קִדְּשָׁנוּ בְּמִצְוֹתָיו,
ve-tsi-va-nu al ne-ti-lat ya-da-yim.	וְצִוָּנוּ עַל נְטִילַת יָדָיִם.

We praise You, Adonai our God, Ruler of the universe, who has made us holy with commandments and commanded us to cleanse our hands.

The Motsi is said as soon as everyone returns to the table.

How is salt used after the Motsi?

After the blessing is said over the challah and the bread has either been cut or broken into pieces, some Jews sprinkle salt on the bread. This is done as a way of comparing the household table to the altar in the historic Jerusalem Temple. As salt was sprinkled on the offerings in Jerusalem, salt can be used on the challah when the meal begins.

When is the word "amen" said?

The word "amen" is first found in the Torah as a response of affirmation. After hearing a series of pronouncements by the Levites (Deuteronomy 27), the Israelites indicate their endorsement of the Levites' words by responding "amen."

"Amen" is used in the same way today. It is said when a person hears someone else say a blessing and then expresses agreement with the sentiments of the blessing by responding "amen."

The Shabbat Meal

Rabbi Judah the Prince made a Shabbat feast for Emperor Antoninus. Though the food was served cold, it was very good. Some time later, the emperor was the host at a feast. Hot dishes were served. At its conclusion, Antoninus said, "The meal you served was better." Judah said, "This meal lacked a particular spice." The emperor was astonished, "Does my treasury lack anything? Tell me what it is, and it shall be purchased." Judah replied, "Shabbat is the spice. It cannot be bought."

Talmud *Shabbat* 119a

In popular culture, Jews are often characterized as a people who like to eat. Although there is a tongue-in-cheek quality to the description of Jews as lovers of food, the connection between Shabbat and food has authentic roots.

In talmudic times, for example, Shabbat was distinguished from the other days of the week (when only two meals were eaten) by the addition of a third meal. The Talmud also describes Shammai the Elder, a first-century B.C.E. sage, whose preparation for Shabbat always involved searching out the finest ingredients for Shabbat dinner. Shammai began the process at the very beginning of the week, but even when he thought he had found the best ingredients, he kept on looking.[12]

For Shammai and Jews during the following centuries, eating well on Shabbat became an important way of honoring Shabbat. The Friday evening meal, along with the two meals during the rest of Shabbat, were each known as a *se-udat mitzvah* (a festive meal accompanying the performance of certain commandments). In the proper context of blessings and ceremonies, then, eating for Jews became a religious obligation. The Friday evening Shabbat dinner, in particular, became a central component of observing Shabbat.

Recipe for the Shabbat Meal

Food

Ashkenazic Jews (Jews of Northern European background) usually associate the Friday evening meal with items such as chicken, chicken soup, gefilte fish, and kugel. Sephardic Jews (Jews of Mediterranean background) include a fish course in their dinner along with rice or beans and possibly lamb. Those who are vegetarians prepare still another Shabbat menu.

Most significantly in our day, all Jews do not necessarily have the time to prepare an elaborate Friday evening dinner. In planning for your own Shabbat meal, therefore, you need not feel constrained to follow any one menu. Especially in the era of dual-career families, it would be better to plan a simple dinner preceded and followed by the blessings than to become overly involved with cooking and baking.

A simple dinner can still be a Shabbat oneg/delight if it includes even one special item such as the first fruit of the new season, a fruit out of season, or a dessert that everyone present will enjoy.

Table conversation

The second ingredient for your Shabbat dinner is table conversation which can try to reflect the holiness of Shabbat. The Talmud says that, just as a person can set aside workday clothes in favor of wearing something out of the ordinary for Shabbat, a person ought to make what is discussed on Shabbat different from other discussions during the week.[13] That should certainly mean reserving conversations about business for other times and trying to focus instead on whatever aspects of our weekly experience relate to us at the fundamental level of our humanity.

Earlier in this book, in the section entitled "Welcoming Shabbat," a list of discussion starters was also given. Although it might at first seem awkward to use these exercises, you may find them useful because they can help focus everyone present on topics they value but might otherwise not approach.

Games

In thinking about the Shabbat meal, it also makes sense to consider what might appeal to children around the Shabbat table. Fortunately, the ceremonies themselves have ready-made appeal. Young children will be delighted to vie for the opportunity to blow out the match after the candles are lit, pour the wine, hold the challah, cut or tear it and then distribute the pieces. In addition, any number of standard children's games can be adapted for use during and after the meal.

Zemirot/Songs

Time after time "music speaks louder than words" and, because of that, music can be a wonderful ingredient in Friday evening's home celebration as well as the rest of Shabbat. *Zemira* (plural, *zemirot*) is the Hebrew word used for the kind of informal song sung around the dinner table. You can find a selection of simple tunes on page 107.

As is the case with so much of the Shabbat ritual, starting is the greatest challenge. If you have never sung at home, it may take some time to convince yourself you can do it. If you have sung only one or two zemirot, you may wonder about learning others. The remedy for your doubts is simple. Just try. Try one or two songs to begin with and you will almost certainly realize that singing together adds a whole new dimension of joy to Shabbat.

Birkat Hamazon
The Blessing after the Meal

You shall eat, be satisfied, and bless Adonai your God for the good land given to you."
Deuteronomy 8:10

As we give thanks to God before the meal, it is also Jewish custom to give thanks with Birkat Hamazon after eating. The component parts of this prayer of gratitude are:

1. PSALM 126—An introductory psalm of hope set at the time when our biblical ancestors returned from exile in Babylonia, Psalm 126 ("A Song of Ascent") is used to introduce Birkat Hamazon only on Shabbat and holidays.

2. ZIMUN / INVITATION — The actual Birkat Hamazon is preceded by a responsive section in which one person acts as leader and invites those present to pray.

3. THE BLESSING FOR FOOD—The first paragraph of Birkat Hamazon expresses thanks to God for providing food.

4. THE BLESSING FOR THE LAND—This paragraph cites the biblical source for Birkat Hamazon (Deuteronomy 8:10). It also thanks God for the Land of Israel.

5. THE BLESSING FOR JERUSALEM—A prayer for the well-being of Jerusalem.

6. ASKING FOR PEACE—A short petition asking that the peace of this one Shabbat fill the whole world.

7. MAKER OF PEACE—The final hope that God bring peace to the world.

If you are not familiar with Hebrew you can begin by doing much of Birkat Hamazon in English. Section 7 of the prayer is probably familiar to many people in Hebrew, so you could end your Birkat Hamazon with this section in Hebrew.

You can find a more extended version of Birkat Hamazon, in which Jewish tradition has elaborated extensively on the themes of sections 4 through 7, in *A Passover Haggadah* (see "Further Reading," page 103).

1. Psalm 126

On Shabbat

♩ See page 113

Shir ha-ma-a-lot.	שִׁיר הַמַּעֲלוֹת.
Be-shuv A-do-nai	בְּשׁוּב יְיָ
et shi-vat Tsi-yon,	אֶת־שִׁיבַת צִיּוֹן,
ha-yi-nu ke-chol-mim.	הָיִינוּ כְּחֹלְמִים.
Az yi-ma-lei se-chok pi-nu,	אָז יִמָּלֵא שְׂחוֹק פִּינוּ,
u-le-sho-nei-nu ri-na.	וּלְשׁוֹנֵנוּ רִנָּה.
Az yom-ru va-goi-yim:	אָז יֹאמְרוּ בַגּוֹיִם:
"Hig-dil A-do-nai la-a-sot im ei-leh."	הִגְדִּיל יְיָ לַעֲשׂוֹת עִם־אֵלֶּה.
Hig-dil A-do-nai la-a-sot i-ma-nu,	הִגְדִּיל יְיָ לַעֲשׂוֹת עִמָּנוּ,
ha-yi-nu se-mei-chim!	הָיִינוּ שְׂמֵחִים!
Shu-va A-do-nai et she-vi-tei-nu	שׁוּבָה יְיָ אֶת־שְׁבִיתֵנוּ
ka-a-fi-kim ba-ne-gev.	כַּאֲפִיקִים בַּנֶּגֶב.
Ha-zor-im be-dim-a,	הַזֹּרְעִים בְּדִמְעָה,
be-ri-na yik-tso-ru.	בְּרִנָּה יִקְצֹרוּ.
Ha-loch yei-leich u-va-cho,	הָלוֹךְ יֵלֵךְ וּבָכֹה,
no-sei me-shech ha-za-ra,	נֹשֵׂא מֶשֶׁךְ־הַזָּרַע,
bo ya-vo ve-ri-na,	בֹּא־יָבֹא בְרִנָּה
no-sei a-lu-mo-tav.	נֹשֵׂא אֲלֻמֹּתָיו.

When God restores the exiled of Zion, we shall be as those who
   dream.
Our mouths will be full of laughter then, our tongues with song.
Then will they say among the nations: "God has done great things
   for them."
God has done great things for us, and so we now rejoice.
Restore us once again, O God, like sudden floodstreams in the
   desert.
Then those who sow in tears will reap in joy.
Those who go forth weeping, bearing the seed for sowing, will
   return bearing the sheaves with song and with laughter.

**2. Zimun /
Invitation**

(On weekdays, begin here)

Leader:
Friends, let us praise God.

Group:

Let the name of God be praised from now to eternity.

Leader:

Let us praise God of whose bounty we have partaken.

Group:

Let us praise our God of whose bounty we have partaken and by whose goodness we live.

Leader:

♪ See page 114

Cha-vei-rai (Ra-bo-tai), *ne-va-reich!*

חֲבֵרַי (רַבּוֹתַי)*, נְבָרֵךְ!

Group:

Ye-hi sheim A-do-nai me-vo-rach
mei-a-ta ve-ad o-lam!

יְהִי שֵׁם יְיָ מְבֹרָךְ
מֵעַתָּה וְעַד עוֹלָם!

Leader:

Ye-hi sheim A-do-nai me-vo-rach
mei-a-ta ve-ad o-lam!
Bi-re-shut cha-vei-rai,
(Bi-re-shut ma-ra-nan
*ve-ra-ba-nan ve-ra-bo-tai)**
*ne-va-reich (E-lo-hei-nu)***
she-a-chal-nu mi-she-lo.

יְהִי שֵׁם יְיָ מְבֹרָךְ
מֵעַתָּה וְעַד עוֹלָם!
בִּרְשׁוּת חֲבֵרַי,
(בִּרְשׁוּת מָרָנָן
וְרַבָּנָן וְרַבּוֹתַי)*
נְבָרֵךְ (אֱלֹהֵינוּ)**
שֶׁאָכַלְנוּ מִשֶּׁלּוֹ.

Group:

*Ba-ruch (E-lo-hei-nu)** she-a-chal-nu*
mi-she-lo u-ve-tu-vo cha-yi-nu.

בָּרוּךְ (אֱלֹהֵינוּ)** שֶׁאָכַלְנוּ
מִשֶּׁלּוֹ וּבְטוּבוֹ חָיִינוּ.

Leader:

*Ba-ruch (E-lo-hei-nu)** she-a-chal-nu*
mi-she-lo u-ve-tu-vo cha-yi-nu.
Ba-ruch hu, u-va-ruch she-mo!

בָּרוּךְ (אֱלֹהֵינוּ)** שֶׁאָכַלְנוּ
מִשֶּׁלּוֹ וּבְטוּבוֹ חָיִינוּ.
בָּרוּךְ הוּא, וּבָרוּךְ שְׁמוֹ!

* Chaveirai, *literally "my friends", is a gender-neutral alternative to the masculine terms traditionally used:* rabotai, *meaning "gentlemen";* maranan, *meaning "masters"; and* rabanan, *meaning "sages."*

**Added when ten or more are present at the meal.*

3. The Blessing for Food

Together:

Ba-ruch a-ta, A-do-nai	בָּרוּךְ אַתָּה, יְיָ
E-lo-hei-nu, me-lech ha-o-lam,	אֱלֹהֵינוּ, מֶלֶךְ הָעוֹלָם,
ha-zan et ha-o-lam	הַזָּן אֶת־הָעוֹלָם
ku-lo be-tu-vo.	כֻּלוֹ בְּטוּבוֹ.
Be-chein be-che-sed u-ve-ra-cha-mim	בְּחֵן בְּחֶסֶד וּבְרַחֲמִים
hu no-tein le-chem	הוּא נוֹתֵן לֶחֶם
le-chol ba-sar,	לְכָל־בָּשָׂר,
ki le-o-lam chas-do.	כִּי לְעוֹלָם חַסְדּוֹ.
U-ve-tu-vo ha-ga-dol	וּבְטוּבוֹ הַגָּדוֹל
ta-mid lo cha-sar la-nu,	תָּמִיד לֹא־חָסַר לָנוּ,
ve-al yech-sar la-nu	וְאַל יֶחְסַר לָנוּ
ma-zon le-o-lam va-ed,	מָזוֹן לְעוֹלָם וָעֶד,
ba-a-vur she-mo ha-ga-dol.	בַּעֲבוּר שְׁמוֹ הַגָּדוֹל.
Ki hu Eil zan u-me-far-neis la-kol	כִּי הוּא אֵל זָן וּמְפַרְנֵס לַכֹּל
u-mei-tiv la-kol	וּמֵטִיב לַכֹּל
u-mei-chin ma-zon	וּמֵכִין מָזוֹן
le-chol be-ri-yo-tav a-sher ba-ra.	לְכָל־בְּרִיּוֹתָיו אֲשֶׁר בָּרָא.
Ba-ruch a-ta, A-do-nai, ha-zan	בָּרוּךְ אַתָּה, יְיָ, הַזָּן
et ha-kol.	אֶת־הַכֹּל.

Through God's kindness, mercy and compassion all existence is eternally sustained. God is forever faithful. God's surpassing goodness fills all time and space. Sustenance there is for all. None need ever lack, no being ever want for food. We praise You, O God, the One sustaining all.

4. The Blessing for the Land

Ka-ka-tuv: "ve-a-chal-ta,	כַּכָּתוּב: וְאָכַלְתָּ
ve-sa-va-ta, u-vei-rach-ta	וְשָׂבָעְתָּ, וּבֵרַכְתָּ
et A-do-nai E-lo-he-cha	אֶת־יְיָ אֱלֹהֶיךָ
al ha-a-rets ha-to-va	עַל־הָאָרֶץ הַטֹּבָה
a-sher na-tan lach."	אֲשֶׁר נָתַן־לָךְ.
Ba-ruch a-ta, A-do-nai,	בָּרוּךְ אַתָּה, יְיָ,
al ha-a-rets ve-al ha-ma-zon.	עַל־הָאָרֶץ וְעַל־הַמָּזוֹן.

As it is written in the Torah: "You shall eat, be satisfied and bless Adonai your God for the good land given to you." We praise You, O God, for the earth and for sustenance.

5. The Blessing for Jerusalem	*U-ve-nei Ye-ru-sha-la-yim*	וּבְנֵה יְרוּשָׁלַיִם
	ir ha-ko-desh	עִיר הַקֹּדֶשׁ
	bi-me-hei-ra ve-ya-mei-nu.	בִּמְהֵרָה בְיָמֵינוּ.
	Ba-ruch a-ta, A-do-nai,	בָּרוּךְ אַתָּה, יְיָ,
	bo-neh ve-ra-cha-mav	בּוֹנֶה בְרַחֲמָיו
	Ye-ru-sha-la-yim. A-mein.	יְרוּשָׁלַיִם. אָמֵן.

And build Jerusalem, O God, speedily in our day. We praise You, O God, whose compassion builds Jerusalem.

---

6. Asking for Peace	**On Shabbat:**	
	Ha-ra-cha-man,	הָרַחֲמָן,
	hu yan-chi-lei-nu	הוּא יַנְחִילֵנוּ
	yom she-ku-lo Sha-bat	יוֹם שֶׁכֻּלּוֹ שַׁבָּת
	u-me nu cha le-cha-yei hu-o-lu-mim.	וּמְנוּחָה לְחַיֵּי הָעוֹלָמִים.

All Merciful, may we inherit a Sabbath of eternal peace.

---

7. Maker of Peace	*O-seh sha-lom bi-me-ro-mav,*	עֹשֶׂה שָׁלוֹם בִּמְרוֹמָיו,
	hu ya-a-seh sha-lom	הוּא יַעֲשֶׂה שָׁלוֹם
	a-lei-nu, ve-al kol Yis-ra-eil,	עָלֵינוּ, וְעַל־כָּל־יִשְׂרָאֵל,
	ve-i-me-ru: A-mein.	וְאִמְרוּ: אָמֵן.

May God who causes peace to reign in the high heavens, bring peace for us and all Israel.

A-do-nai oz le-a-mo yi-tein,	יְיָ עֹז לְעַמּוֹ יִתֵּן,
A-do-nai ye-va-reich	יְיָ יְבָרֵךְ
et a-mo va-sha-lom.	אֶת־עַמּוֹ בַשָּׁלוֹם.

May God give strength to our people. May God bless all peoples with peace.

Who wrote Birkat Hamazon?

Birkat Hamazon is largely a creation of the rabbis whose lives and work are described in the Mishnah and Talmud. These post-biblical texts came into being during the first five centuries of the Common Era and they represent the attempt of the scholar-leaders of Judaism to clarify Jewish practice.

The Mishnah is the first Jewish text to mention the custom of reciting a blessing after eating. Short examples of the prayer resembling the Zimun/Invitation of today are recorded.[14]

Later texts in the Talmud indicate how the Birkat Hamazon became an increasingly complex repository of material. Giving thanks for food became the occasion for giving thanks for the covenant, the land of Israel, and the hope of future redemption.

Does the Torah mention Birkat Hamazon?

No, it doesn't. It does, however, contain Deuteronomy 8:10, which reads: "You shall eat, be satisfied, and bless Adonai...." Although we do not know if this verse gave rise to a blessing after meals in biblical times, we do know that by the time of the Rabbis this verse was considered to be the biblical rationale for Birkat Hamazon. Deuteronomy 8:10 is the only Torah verse quoted in full in the Birkat Hamazon (see "The Blessing for the Land," page 36).

How important is Birkat Hamazon?

Although it can be difficult to refocus those at the table after they have eaten, Birkat Hamazon should definitely be included in your home service. It is, after all, the component of the service with the most direct connection to the Torah.

It is also the only table prayer that explicitly presents a messianic vision (see "Asking for Peace" and "Maker of Peace"). Since Shabbat is often described as a foretaste of the perfected future, Birkat Hamazon is important because it actively expresses that hope for a compassionate and peaceful world.

Despite this, you may still need to make an extra effort in order to integrate Birkat Hamazon into your Shabbat. You can help the process along by reminding everyone at your table that after eating and singing, you *do* want to conclude with Birkat Hamazon. Doing an abbreviated version of the prayer (try sections 3 and 7) can also ease you into the routine.

Erev Shabbat and Shabbat Day in the Synagogue

May my prayer come to You, God, at an acceptable time.
Psalms 69:14

When is the time acceptable? When the community is at prayer.
Talmud *Berachot* 8a

Going Beyond the Home

If you have already read about or experienced Friday evening's home service, you are ready for the next step in exploring Shabbat.

That involves remembering that welcoming Shabbat at home is merely a beginning. Just as the opening cadence of a symphony can be magnificent, but still only hints at what lies beyond, Friday evening's dinner only welcomes Shabbat. The home experience sets the stage for what is yet to come during the rest of Shabbat.

And what is yet to come is the synagogue. The opportunity to pray, to study, and to meet the broader community of Jews is all available in the synagogue.

Of course, to go to the synagogue a Jew has to leave home, which in our world is not always simple. There is the thrust in contemporary culture toward a privatism that invites us to retreat into our homes and families. We are easily inclined to focus in on ourselves and an immediate circle of relationships as opposed to looking outward to the world around.

Besides that, if Shabbat begins to appeal to you as a respite from weekday pressures, it can almost seem contradictory to create a sense of sanctuary at home and then head for the public sanctuary in the synagogue. However, Judaism does ask you to do just this. Judaism asks that Jews make space in their lives for sanctifying acts in the communal home of the synagogue as well as in their private homes.

Something unique and complementary to Shabbat at home happens in the synagogue. You will discover it when you go beyond your home to enter the synagogue.

Going Inside the Synagogue

For most people the word "synagogue" is synonymous with services. To a large extent, the common perception is true. The synagogue has historically been known as a Beit Tefila/House of Prayer. But that is not all, because the synagogue has also had at least two other names over the centuries—Beit Midrash/House of Study and Beit Keneset/House of Assembly.

There have been three names for the synagogue because the synagogue has been a multifaceted institution in Jewish life offering prayer, study, and, in the midst of it all, an opportunity for communal gathering.

Your involvement in this truly three-dimensional institution can, therefore, take place at many different levels. As some aspects of the Friday evening home service may speak to you more than others, different aspects of the synagogue's life may also attract you.

Beit Tefila/House of Prayer

To begin with, you can pray in the synagogue. True, you need not be in a synagogue in order to have prayerful thoughts. You do not even need a prayerbook with its fixed prayers to have a spiritual experience.

Nevertheless, Jews maintain synagogues, print common prayerbooks, and schedule regular times for community prayer because of the special way we understand reality. For us, the operative pronoun is "we." Virtually every ceremony and prayer uses language in the plural because our commitment to the autonomy of every human being is balanced by the belief that the individual Jew is always part of a larger community. Just as certain prayers are not generally said in the absence of a minyan/quorum, we believe that being a Jew involves living with a sense of belonging to the broader world around us.

We fix times for praying together because, as Rabbi Eugene Borowitz writes, "Group prayer, by confronting us with others, by asking us to link our prayers to theirs, reminds us immediately and directly that it is never enough to pray for ourselves alone." We share the same needs and desires as others. We are private selves and, at the same time, members of humanity.

Therefore, the goal is that, having celebrated personal and family ties around a private dinner table, you will next move into the synagogue in order to confirm the connections that take you beyond your private world.

When you open the prayerbook, you will feel drawn into the drama of the world surrounding us all. When you help form a community of praying Jews, you will come to feel the connections between yourself and Jews around the globe reciting and singing similar words in their synagogues.

Finally, Jews pray in the synagogue because prayer accomplishes one other important purpose: it enables us to step away from the material, weekday world. If the six days of the week force us to concern ourselves with results and the "bottom line," the prayerbook is important because it reminds us that human beings have an upper reach as well.

Praying brings us into a realm where we consider the great questions of purpose and value in life. Through prayer we open ourselves up to God and the hope that God will support us in our search for meaning even as God challenges us to look within ourselves and strengthen our finest human impulses.

As Rabbi Abraham Joshua Heschel taught, prayer can help accomplish the larger purpose of Shabbat, which is "to turn from the results of creation, to the mystery of creation; from the world of creation, to the creation of the world."

Beit Midrash/House of Study

Inside the synagogue you can also study. Indeed, the opportunity to read and study the Torah portion of the week in the synagogue has always been one of the highlights of Shabbat.

Jews call the Torah a "tree of life" and lavish attention on its meaning because the Torah and the great Jewish texts based on it provide the underpinnings for Judaism's beliefs, practices, and values.

The Mishnah describes the importance of the Torah in these words: "Turn it, turn it, for everything is in it."[15]

The Talmud presents Torah study in this way: "These are the obligations without measure, whose reward, too, is without measure—to honor father and mother; to perform acts of love and kindness; to attend the house of study daily; to welcome the stranger; to visit the sick; to rejoice with bride and groom; to console the bereaved; to pray with sincerity; to make peace when there is strife. *And the study of Torah is equal to them all because it leads to them all.*"[16]

The end result of this perspective is that any synagogue you enter on Shabbat will offer you an opportunity to deepen your knowledge of the Torah and related Jewish texts. You may encounter a Torah-oriented sermon or discussion during the evening or morning service. On Shabbat morning, you may find a separate study group.

Most importantly, if you take the journey into the texts of our people, your whole sense of Judaism stands to gain. Through study you will begin to grasp the breadth and depth of Judaism. You will come to understand more about the customs and ceremonies you practice.

As you continue to learn, your understanding of why it even matters to live Jewishly will also develop. The more you know about Judaism the more compelling you will find its teachings.

Beit Keneset/House of Assembly

One other aspect of the synagogue is experienced on Shabbat. It is the experience of the synagogue as a place where Jews meet other Jews.

Next to all the weighty issues raised in presenting the synagogue as a place for prayer and study, simply bringing Jews together may seem to be beside the point. Nevertheless, the synagogue has been appreciated by Jews over the years as an important place of assembly. The English word "synagogue" even comes from the Greek *synagoge*, which is a literal translation of the term, Beit Keneset/House of Assembly.

You cannot be a Jew in a vacuum. Judaism is a "group faith," which is to say that, in addition to the personal religious experience each of us may have as Jews, we can also share a sense of historic and communal connectedness. We do that by being with other Jews; we do that by appreciating the synagogue as a house of assembly.

This book uses the word "synagogue" all the time. I thought Reform Jews went to "temple." Is there a difference in meaning between the two terms?

Although the terms are often used interchangeably, a meaningful distinction can be drawn between them. When studying Jewish history, "Temple" is the word used for the building in Jerusalem where our ancestors worshipped primarily through sacrifices. The First Temple was built by King Solomon and destroyed by the Babylonians four centuries later in 586 B.C.E. The Second Temple, begun some fifty years later, was destroyed by the Romans in 70 C.E.

During the Second Temple period an institution called the synagogue began to emerge. The synagogue was different from the Temple in that sacrifices did not take place there. Instead, the synagogue provided a setting for prayer by words. With the destruction of the Second Temple, the synagogue went on to become the central institution of the Jewish community where prayer and study were the focus.

When Reform Judaism began in the nineteenth century, the pioneers of the movement wanted to identify their new approach to Jewish life and prayer by using a new term for their houses of worship. The term they used to describe their synagogues was "temple." They liked the term because it suggested that, although the historic Temple in Jerusalem was gone, the modern Reform synagogue was its worthy successor.

In our time the term "temple" has mostly lost its ideological overtones. It remains as the title many Reform and Conservative congregations take for their synagogue.

Does the Friday evening service always follow Shabbat dinner?

No, it does not. In many traditional Jewish settings worshippers (usually male) would assemble at the synagogue as the sun was about to set. While women were at home preparing for dinner and lighting the Shabbat candles, the men would participate in a service called "Kabbalat Shabbat," which means "welcoming Shabbat."

After the Kabbalat Shabbat service the worshippers would return home and spend the rest of the evening there.

When Reform Judaism began to develop in Europe and North America, one of the early areas of concern had to do with Shabbat observance. Out of an interest in raising attendance at Shabbat services, several American rabbis in the 1860's experimented with a later Friday evening service. Over time the post-dinner Shabbat service has become the norm in Reform Judaism, although some Reform congregations also schedule regular or at least periodic pre-dinner Kabbalat Shabbat services.

If Friday evening's Shabbat dinner fills our home with the spirit of Shabbat, is it possible to stay home in order to hold onto this spirit?

Some Reform congregations are now experimenting with several variations in Shabbat synagogue attendance. They are doing so in order to allow congregants to capture the best of what Shabbat offers in both the home and the synagogue.

For example, in communities where the pre-dinner Kabbalat Shabbat service exists, congregants are encouraged to attend this service and then go home in order to eat together and spend the rest of the evening in each other's company.

Other congregations de-emphasize the late Friday evening service by following the traditional practice of making their Saturday morning service into the main Shabbat service. In these synagogues congregants are encouraged to make Friday evening their home experience and Saturday morning their community experience.

If the candlelighting and Kiddush are done at home Friday evening, why are they also done during the synagogue Evening Service?

Candlelighting in the synagogue is a fairly recent innovation of Reform Judaism, although there may have been some Jewish communities in the past that also had Shabbat candlelighting in the synagogue. Rav Amram Gaon, a ninth-century Babylonian sage, records that, in his time, after entering the synagogue on Friday afternoon and reciting the Afternoon Service, "one who kindles the Sabbath lights must recite the benediction."

The practice of reciting Kiddush in the synagogue as well as in the home has been common throughout the Jewish world since talmudic times. In those days the synagogue was frequently used as a place for travelers to eat and sleep, and the custom of reciting Kiddush in the synagogue was begun for the benefit of these people.[17] It was understood that saying Kiddush in the synagogue was not a substitute for saying it in one's own home.

What are the origins of the Oneg Shabbat?

The phrase "Oneg Shabbat," which means "Sabbath joy," derives from the prophet Isaiah who urged the Jewish people in his time to "call Shabbat a delight." (Isaiah 58:13)

In recent times Oneg Shabbat has come to refer to the social hour that follows Shabbat evening services. The idea of using the term Oneg Shabbat as the title for a specific component of Shabbat originated with the Hebrew poet Chaim Nachman Bialik (1873–1934). Bialik used to convene a Shabbat afternoon gathering that consisted of discussion, singing, refreshments, and Havdalah. He called his gathering an "Oneg Shabbat." In due course, the new term came to be applied as it is now.

When did the custom of a public Torah reading arise?

The sources available to historians do not permit exact dating for the origin of this practice. However, just as the synagogue began to emerge during the period of the Second Temple, scholars believe that the institution of a public Torah reading also developed during this era.

By the end of the second century C.E., the public reading of the Torah appears to have been well established. Thus the Mishnah mentions Monday, Thursday, and Shabbat as regular times for reading the Torah. The Mishnah also specifies portions of the Torah that are to be read for the Jewish holidays.[18] The first reference to the kind of fixed cycle of consecutive Torah readings that is followed today occurs in a talmudic text.[19]

A final thought on the significance of the weekly Shabbat Torah readings.

Franz Rosenzweig was a leading theologian and teacher among German Jews during the 1920's. In his major book on Judaism, *The Star of Redemption*, he presented this understanding of the relationship between Shabbat and the cycle for the reading of the Torah.

"In the circle of weekly portions which, in the course of one year, cover all of the Torah, the spiritual year is paced out, and the paces of this course are the Sabbaths. By and large, every Sabbath is just like any other, but the difference in the portions from the Scriptures distinguishes each from each, and this difference shows that they are not final in themselves but only parts of a higher order of the year. For only in the year do the differentiating elements of the individual parts again fuse into a whole....It is only in the sequence of the Sabbaths that the year rounds to a garland."

Shabbat Day
The Home Service

Shabbat Day
The Home Service

The Prophet Isaiah says, "And you shall call the Sabbath a delight." How does a person express joy on Shabbat? By eating even the smallest amount of food as long as it is prepared in honor of Shabbat.

Talmud Shabbat 118b

As much as Shabbat liberates a Jew from the scheduling and goal-oriented style of the weekday, Shabbat itself still has a definite structure. There are specific ways to welcome the day, fixed times for prayer and study, and special ways to celebrate the meals.

Thus, the talmudic rabbis gave the midday meal that followed services on Saturday morning its own unique Shabbat status. A modified Kiddush was developed for this meal, challah was eaten again, and the custom of singing zemirot/songs after the meal was also carried over from Friday evening.

In this context we now present the specific Kiddush for Shabbat morning. Many congregations recite this Kiddush following their Shabbat morning service. In your home it can be the introduction to a leisurely lunch that shares the same spirit as Friday evening's dinner.

Kiddush

Shabbat and the
Covenant

Raise the Kiddush cups filled with wine or grape juice.

Ve-sha-me-ru ve-nei Yis-ra-eil	וְשָׁמְרוּ בְנֵי־יִשְׂרָאֵל
et ha-sha-bat,	אֶת־הַשַּׁבָּת,
la-a-sot et ha-sha-bat	לַעֲשׂוֹת אֶת־הַשַּׁבָּת
le-do-ro-tam be-rit o-lam.	לְדֹרֹתָם בְּרִית עוֹלָם.
Bei-ni u-vein be-nei Yis-ra-eil	בֵּינִי וּבֵין בְּנֵי יִשְׂרָאֵל
ot hi le-o-lam,	אוֹת הִיא לְעֹלָם,
ki shei-shet ya-mim a-sa A-do-nai	כִּי שֵׁשֶׁת יָמִים עָשָׂה יְיָ
et ha-sha-ma-yim ve-et ha-a-rets,	אֶת־הַשָּׁמַיִם וְאֶת־הָאָרֶץ,
u-va-yom ha-she-vi-i	וּבַיּוֹם הַשְּׁבִיעִי
sha-vat va-yi-na-fash.	שָׁבַת וַיִּנָּפַשׁ.

The people of Israel shall keep Shabbat, observing Shabbat in
every generation as a covenant for all time. It shall be a sign for
ever between Me and the people of Israel, for in six days God
made heaven and earth, and on the seventh day God rested and
was refreshed.

(Exodus 31:16–17)

Al kein bei-rach A-do-nai	עַל־כֵּן בֵּרַךְ יְיָ
et yom ha-sha-bat va-ye-ka-de-shei-hu.	אֶת־יוֹם הַשַּׁבָּת וַיְקַדְּשֵׁהוּ.

Therefore, Adonai blessed the seventh day and called it holy.

Blessing over the
Wine

♪ See page 118
("Havdalah
Blessings")

Ba-ruch a-ta, A-do-nai	בָּרוּךְ אַתָּה, יְיָ
E-lo-hei-nu, me-lech ha-o-lam,	אֱלֹהֵינוּ, מֶלֶךְ הָעוֹלָם,
bo-rei pe-ri ha-ga-fen.	בּוֹרֵא פְּרִי הַגָּפֶן.

We praise You, Adonai, our God, Ruler of the universe, Creator of
the fruit of the vine.

Blessing over the Bread

🎼 See page 113

After drinking the wine, recite the Motsi.

Ba-ruch a-ta, A-do-nai

E-lo-hei-nu, me-lech ha-o-lam,

ha-mo-tsi le-chem min ha-a-rets.

בָּרוּךְ אַתָּה, יְיָ

אֱלֹהֵינוּ, מֶלֶךְ הָעוֹלָם,

הַמּוֹצִיא לֶחֶם מִן הָאָרֶץ.

We praise You, Adonai our God, Ruler of the universe, who brings forth bread from the earth.

Distribute and eat pieces of the challah.

(Birkat Hamazon and zemirot/songs conclude the meal as they did on Friday evening. See pages 34 and 107.)

What distinguishes the Shabbat morning Kiddush from the Friday evening Kiddush?

Unlike the Friday evening Kiddush, which consists of both the one-line blessing over the wine plus the paragraph that sanctifies the day of Shabbat, the Shabbat morning Kiddush is more compact. According to the Talmud,[20] it originally consisted of only the blessing for the wine. In later times a number of biblical passages were added to the morning Kiddush in order to introduce the blessing. Our text uses Exodus 31:16–17 for this purpose.

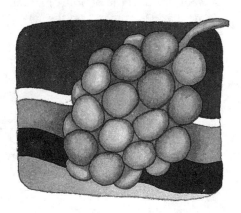

Establishing Definitions for Work and Rest on Shabbat

For the contemporary Jew who wants to observe Shabbat, there is probably no greater challenge than maintaining the spirit of Shabbat beyond Saturday morning.*

The problem is that if you have already made Kiddush, sung the various songs, and been in synagogue to pray and study (or even if you haven't managed to follow Shabbat thus far), your next step is not a given. That is because, on Saturday afternoon, you enter a time period without prescribed rituals. To sustain the mood of Friday evening and Saturday, you therefore cannot fall back on the performance of ceremonies.

Instead, you are left to address the basic premise of the seventh day, which is that it is supposed to be "a day of rest." This means that if you want Shabbat to be different from other days, Saturday afternoon becomes the time for deciding what you can do beyond ceremony in order to make the concept of rest a reality.

To do this, you need to remember that Jewish tradition means something quite specific when it uses the term "rest" in connection with Shabbat.

Resting on Shabbat doesn't involve merely taking the day off or sleeping late. The *absence* of activity alone does not create Shabbat. On the contrary, Shabbat is very much associated with involvement in friendship, community, prayer, and study. The day that brings "rest" and peace is potentially full of stimulation.

So what, then, does Jewish tradition mean when it directs us to "rest" on the seventh day?

Jewish tradition says very little about the nature of that rest. Instead, it emphasizes the opposite—it specifies in detail what activities are not appropriate for Shabbat. These activities are defined as melacha/work, and are explained at the end of this section. You can see there how, under the category of "work," the tradition goes to great lengths to prohibit numerous activities which are perceived to be intrusions on the spirit of the seventh day.

Apparently, the sages who first grappled with the meaning of Shabbat rest decided that their primary task was to create some open space in the week in

---

* Although the issues raised in this section of *Shaarei Shabbat* are applicable to the unstructured time period of Saturday afternoon, they also pertain throughout Shabbat. For example, depending on the definition of work and rest, one Jew may or may not watch television at some point on Friday evening. Another Jew may or may not drive to temple. Defining rest and work is at the heart of Shabbat observance. The criteria for arriving at such definitions are established in this section.

order to let rest take place. Like foresters who want to clear an opening in the forest, the sages took the Torah's injunction against work on Shabbat and used it to build a fence that held back anything resembling weekday occupations and diversions.

Shabbat became the protected clearing within the week when whatever was not work could blossom.

If you are now ready to move forward with your own Shabbat observance, this is the scenario you face in defining "rest." On the one hand, you need to respond to the thrust in Judaism that prohibits "work." You must consider which weekday activities traditionally prohibited on Shabbat you will avoid.

On the other hand, you need to ask yourself what you will do to fill the space created by the abstentions that you make. What will you do *positively* on Shabbat in order to keep the spirit of the day alive?

This section of *Shaarei Shabbat* is designed to help you respond to these questions about rest and work. When you read through the examples and especially when you try to apply the categories of work and rest to your own Shabbat, you will find yourself trying to resolve the tension between what you will and will not do on Shabbat. You will also be dealing with the tension between treating free time on Shabbat like free time on any other day as opposed to making free time on Shabbat into something unique. These very worthwhile tensions are the creative dynamic out of which you can fashion your Shabbat observance.

Three Jews—Three Models for Work and Rest on Shabbat

Three examples culled from the lives of many Reform Jews point the way.*

The Walker

In six days Adonai made heaven and earth and sea, and all that is in them, and rested on the seventh day; therefore Adonai blessed Shabbat and sanctified it.
The Shabbat commandment in Exodus 20:11

Imagine a Jew whose approach to Shabbat is strongly influenced by the desire to establish a totally separate realm of activity for the seventh day.

He or she grounds this view of Shabbat in the Friday evening Kiddush, which concludes with the idea that the seventh day ought to be a "sanctified" day. It should be a day with an element of kedusha/holiness. According to the

* In order to be as clear as possible about the decision-making process which goes into defining Shabbat "rest," the models in this section have been presented as individuals without the sometimes conflicting responsibilities of family. Part of the challenge involved in bringing these theoretical constructs to life involves placing yourself into the real social network of spouse, children, and friends.

intent of the Hebrew, this means Shabbat is a day that ought to be "set aside." What is done on Shabbat should have the feeling of being holy because it is clearly different from what happens on a Wednesday or a Sunday.

With all this in mind, consider the example of the walker. He or she does not pursue his or her occupation on Shabbat. The walker is a Jew who makes the seventh day holy by choosing not to use the car and not to spend or even carry money on Shabbat. The walker puts aside these so-called necessities of modern life and uses Shabbat afternoon, in particular, as a time for taking walks, private reading, studying with a group of friends, picnicking, or any activity along these lines.

What the walker does on Shabbat afternoon is a total change of pace from anything done on other days. It means doing something positive through thought, leisure, and friendship while it also involves choosing from among the various Shabbat abstentions in rabbinic literature to avoid what Jewish tradition has come to call "work" on Shabbat.

Why do that at all? Why withdraw from money or the automobile? On the same principle, why might another Reform Jew make the seventh day holy by avoiding the telephone, the television or home computer? Why seek kedusha/holiness in these ways?

The Torah offers a rationale for the withdrawal by calling on Jews to observe Shabbat because it is a reminder that "in six days Adonai made heaven and earth...and rested on the seventh day...and sanctified it." (Exodus 20:11) Since God had no need to rest because of physical fatigue, what can God's resting mean? It teaches us that, as God stopped creating and manipulating the physical world on the seventh day, we ought to do the same.

The walker withdraws from the tools of civilization, acknowledging that the world is not our human creation. It functions by itself, and we leave it to do so on Shabbat in order to focus on ourselves instead of everything but ourselves, our values, and our goals.

As Rabbi Abraham Joshua Heschel taught, "Six days a week we seek to dominate the world, on the seventh day we try to dominate the self." On Shabbat we leave the material world to search for wholeness in the inner world of self, friends, and family.

The Museumgoer

> *In six days God made heaven and earth, and on the seventh day*
> *God rested and was refreshed.*
>
> Exodus 31:17

Imagine now a second Jew who also stays away from business on Shabbat. Unlike the walker, however, this Jew will spend money and drive on Shabbat, although he or she limits the use of money or the automobile to certain activities that he or she feels are appropriate for the creation of a meaningful Shabbat. This Jew doesn't drive to the mall in order to shop on Shabbat, but *will* go to a museum.

How does the museumgoer draw a distinction between spending money to enter the museum as opposed to purchasing a new lamp at the mall?

The museumgoer would say that spending money on Shabbat is not the issue, as much as it is *how* one spends money that matters. In this case, the museumgoer is approaching Shabbat as a day of freedom from necessity. As busy as he or she is all week long, the joy of Shabbat for the museumgoer lies in the fact that on Shabbat he or she doesn't respond to the pressure of running errands. He or she doesn't use Saturday's free time in order to do what could be done on a longer lunch hour or a mere day off.

For the museumgoer Saturday afternoon becomes Shabbat when it is devoted to activities that are ends in themselves.

And Saturday can feel even more like Shabbat when the activities in question involve family or friends for whom there is so little time during the rest of the week. The joy of Shabbat comes into play when, at least once a week, the museumgoer can spend time for its own sake with the people he or she cares about most. On the seventh day, the museumgoer rests (in accordance with Exodus 31:17) by seeking out the kinds of activities that refresh and give new life to the soul.

By the way, on those Shabbat afternoons when the museum is closed, the museumgoer does have other options. He can ski; she can go to the beach. And what makes these leisure activities on Shabbat different from the same activity on other days of the week is that the committed Reform Jew thinks differently about them. They are done intentionally, *lichvod Shabbat*, in honor of Shabbat.

The museumgoer can run errands and do laundry or join the family at the movies on Sunday. By way of contrast, the beauty of Shabbat is the feeling that, on Saturday, the choice between housework and family does not apply.

Shabbat is by definition a no-errand, no-chore day. Leisure or "rest" is the only refreshing option on Shabbat.

The Painter

Remember that you were a slave in the land of Egypt and Adonai your God freed you from there…therefore Adonai your God has commanded you to observe Shabbat.

The Shabbat commandment in Deuteronomy 5:15

For both the walker and museumgoer, resolving the tension between what a Jew should not do on Shabbat (work) as opposed to what a Jew should do (rest) is the essential issue in finding a path through Shabbat afternoon.

In fact, as different as the walker and museumgoer may be, each would agree with Mordecai Kaplan who draws an analogy between art and life.

Kaplan writes that, as an artist periodically puts down his brush in order to refresh his perspective on his creation, Shabbat represents the weekly time in life "when we pause in our brushwork to renew our vision."

For the walker and the museumgoer, the pause is fundamental. Indeed, the Shabbat pause has to have a certain quality. Shabbat is not only a day to avoid business as usual. It is also a day to avoid leisure as usual, which means that whether they are talking, strolling, or swimming, both Jews see Shabbat as a time for truly letting go of the world-as-usual.

They "put down the paintbrush" and rest on Shabbat by trying to interfere as little as possible with the equilibrium of the world as it exists when the sun sets on Friday. After six days of creating or contributing to the world, on the seventh day the walker and museumgoer try not to engage in the creative process at all.

Imagine a third Jew, however, who does something very different when he or she puts down the figurative paintbrush of the work week. Imagine that Jew walking away from his computer terminal or closing her ledger books and then literally picking up a paintbrush on Shabbat afternoon in order to create a work of art.

When other Jews believe that Shabbat ought to mean avoiding the creative process, how can the painter claim to be observing Shabbat?

The painter's claim derives from the Shabbat commandment as it appears in the Book of Deuteronomy. In those verses the Torah describes Shabbat as a reminder of the Exodus from Egypt. For the painter, the Book of Deuteronomy would be teaching that Shabbat is best observed when it calls to mind the end of Egyptian slavery and the gift of freedom that came with it. Shabbat would, therefore, be a day on which we remember our ancestors' liberation by allowing ourselves to feel liberated as well.

What activities might liberate contemporary people whose days are filled with meetings, appointments, and errands? Painting might be just the antidote for that lifestyle because it involves such a totally different perspective on life. For that matter, any creative endeavor might also bring a breath of fresh air into our lives. It would be a Shabbat activity if it were an activity we didn't pursue on the other days of the week. It would be appropriate to Shabbat afternoon if it helped us refocus ourselves after a week of errands or wage-earning.

For some Jews, finding an activity that liberated them from the mundane could be the essence of "rest" on Shabbat. It could allow their weekday minds and spirits to "rest" as hands and body came into play in ways that are impossible all through the week.

Your Decision: How Will You Establish a Definition for Work and Rest on Shabbat?

The walker, the museumgoer, and the painter have all made their choices for Shabbat, and the choices vary greatly. They run the gamut from traditional definitions of rest on Shabbat to definitions that appear to be altogether untraditional.

Most importantly, each definition of rest given here has its own validity. The walker, the museumgoer, and the painter are authentic Reform Jews because the decisions they reach are made with sincerity, commitment, and a desire to draw on the resources of Judaism in order to enrich contemporary life. One Jew may weigh the various aspects of Shabbat differently than does another —he or she may emphasize liberation more than separation. Another stresses family connectedness for the sake of Shabbat joy and shapes Shabbat to achieve that goal.

What counts most is that each Jew wants to make Saturday into Shabbat and thoughtfully finds a way to do so. Each of the three draws on Jewish tradition to create a Shabbat that is true to the spirit of the day.

The next step

As a reader of this guide, the next step is now yours.

In order to develop your definitions for work and rest on Shabbat, you should do the following:

A. Study the discussion and models that opened this section, along with the material that follows here and in the section of "Readings and Meditations."

B. Remember two things about the models in this section. First, the models are only theoretical. They are teaching devices offering you a way for beginning to think about work and rest as you move toward your own observance. You can draw on all or part of any of the models in your decision-making.

Secondly, remember that the three models in this section do not exist in a vacuum. This book is not suggesting that a family day at the beach constitutes Shabbat or that painting or museumgoing are in and of themselves Shabbat activities. They must be part of a larger whole that takes its shape from the home and synagogue ceremonies described throughout Shaarei Shabbat.

What might otherwise merely be a leisure activity becomes an expression of Shabbat when it is consciously done in order to complement the sacred acts (from candlelighting to Havdalah) that are part of Jewish tradition.

C. Finally, when it actually comes to choosing Shabbat activities, consider these six questions. They can be the criteria which you weigh in deciding if a given activity is or is not appropriate for Shabbat afternoon.

Ask yourself:

1. Will this activity lend Shabbat a quality of kedusha/holiness?
2. Is this activity done for its own sake or is it merely a means to an end?
3. Does this activity imbue Shabbat with a sense of liberation?
4. Does this activity help cultivate a sense of wonder at God's creation?
5. Does this activity advance the spirit of Shabbat embodied in the home and synagogue celebrations of the seventh day?
6. Does this activity bring me closer to the Jewish people?

More Thoughts on the Meaning of "Work" and "Rest"

The day of rest has become a day of busy work

In our Western culture the day of rest has now become another day of busy work, filled with amusements and restless diversions not essentially different from the routine of the work week, particularly in America. From the Sunday morning scramble through the metropolitan newspapers, to the distracting tedium of the motor car excursion, we continuously activate leisure time, instead of letting all work and routine duties come serenely to a halt.

Lewis Mumford

Shabbat as protest

I view the Sabbath...as a "useless" day. We must once again understand that doing nothing, being silent and open to the world, letting things happen inside, can be as important as, and sometimes more important than, what we commonly call the useful. Let there be some special time during the week when we do for the sake of doing, when we love the trivial and, in fact, simply love; when we do for others rather than ourselves and thus provide a counter-balance for the weight of endless competition that burdens our every day.

W. Gunther Plaut

It takes real effort

The "work" that is forbidden by Jewish law on the Sabbath is not measured in the expenditure of energy. It takes real effort to pray, to study, to walk to synagogue. They are "rest" but not restful. Forbidden "work" is acquisition, aggrandizement, altering the world. On Shabbat we are obliged to be, to reflect, to love and make love, to eat, to enjoy.

Arnold Jacob Wolf

Being fully aware

[The Sabbath means] being fully aware of the apple tree but having no judgments, plans, or prospects for it.

Harvey Cox

❖

It is permissible to make plans for good deeds on the Sabbath...one may arrange alms to the poor on Sabbath....One may transact business which has to do with the saving of life or with public health on Sabbath, and one may go to synagogue to discuss public affairs on Sabbath....

Talmud *Shabbat* 150a

Reform Judaism clearly allows for a broad definition of work and rest on Shabbat. What is the position on work and rest of the halacha/legal system of traditional Judaism?

The injunction against melacha/work on Shabbat is presented several times in the Torah. For example, in the context of the Ten Commandments, the Torah says, "Six days you shall labor and do all your work but the seventh day is a Sabbath of Adonai your God: you shall not do any work." (Exodus 20:9–10, Deuteronomy 5:13–14)

Although the meaning of this commandment seems clear, the rabbis who actually tried to apply the commandment found that neither Exodus 20 nor Deuteronomy 5 was specific about the kinds of work forbidden on Shabbat.

That is not to say that the Torah and the rest of the Bible are silent about activities that violate Shabbat. Kindling a flame, plowing, harvesting and reaping, gathering wood, baking and cooking, carrying a burden or carrying something out of the house, and buying and selling are all prohibited on Shabbat.[21]

Despite this, the desire to elaborate on the specific meaning of the term melacha/work led the rabbis to develop a system in the Mishnah and Talmud consisting of no fewer than thirty-nine categories of work (see page 75) plus innumerable secondary categories derived from them. In addition, other kinds of activities were to be avoided because they were not in the spirit of Shabbat.

The source of the thirty-nine major categories lies in the Torah's juxtaposition of some laws regarding Shabbat (Exodus 35: 1–3) with the description of the construction of the portable sanctuary begun at Mount Sinai. The fact that the Shabbat laws immediately precede the construction suggested to the rabbis that the term melacha/work should cover the kinds of activities performed in constructing this sanctuary.[22]

These activities included work in the field (plowing, sowing, reaping, threshing, etc.), preparation of food (grinding, kneading, baking, slaughtering, hunting), preparation of clothing (sheep-shearing, dyeing, spinning, sewing), and writing.

Basing itself on the Talmud, later Jewish legal literature has continued to define the meaning of work on Shabbat. In modern times, this has involved dealing with such matters as the use of electricity and the automobile.

Why does the Reform approach to Shabbat work and rest differ from that of traditional Judaism?

Reform Jews depart from the traditional definitions of work and rest because we believe that they do not represent the final word on Jewish practice. We maintain that the talmudic sages and their successors only developed definitions of work and rest in response to the specific historic needs of the Jews they knew. The sages themselves even acknowledged that much of their Shabbat legislation was only loosely related to the Torah.[23] Nevertheless, they continued refining their ideas of Shabbat because the biblical Shabbat had to be clarified and elucidated if it was to be followed in their post-biblical world.

The same holds true for us today. We are "commanded," as it were, to continue what Jews have done for centuries. We must develop definitions of work and rest that resonate with the needs of contemporary Jews.

One caveat needs to be stated. In creating a contemporary approach to Shabbat, Reform Jews do not function in a vacuum. Although we may depart from ancient practices, we live with a sense of responsibility to the continuum of Jewish experience.

Therefore, we try to balance our creativity in practice with the desire to conserve and adapt what speaks to us from the past. We are free to be novel, but proud as well to maintain as much as possible our connections with the best of the Jewish past.

Does Reform Judaism have a position on the specific matter of pursuing one's occupation on Shabbat?

Reform Jewish sources affirm the principle that a person should not pursue his or her gainful occupation on Shabbat. In the first edition of the *Shabbat Manual*, Rabbi W. Gunther Plaut wrote: "Reform Judaism...upholds the principle that proper Shabbat observance calls for cessation from unnecessary work and business activity."

Rabbi Plaut also affirmed Reform Judaism's acceptance of the reality that circumstances can sometimes make it impossible for a person to avoid work. In such cases a Reform Jew is advised to participate in as many observances of Shabbat as possible.

What does Reform Judaism say about scheduling or attending private or public events such as parties or school functions on Friday evenings and Saturdays?

The observance of Shabbat requires us not to schedule or attend private or communal events that prevent participation in Shabbat. If Friday night is the time for welcoming Shabbat, it should be treated differently than any other night of the week. The same holds true for Saturday. If it is to be experienced as Shabbat, Saturday should be reserved for the kinds of activities described in this guide.

Should life-cycle ceremonies be scheduled on Shabbat?

BERIT MILA / THE COVENANT OF CIRCUMCISION—In Genesis (17:11–12), the Torah first mentions circumcision for Jewish male children. Because these verses so clearly link circumcision to the eighth day of the child's life, the berit mila ceremony takes place on the eighth day even if that day falls on Shabbat. Circumcision may be postponed for medical reasons, although it should be rescheduled as soon as the child is healthy.

Since some modern covenant or baby-naming ceremonies for female children follow the model of berit mila by being connected to the eighth day, they should also be conducted on that day even if it is Shabbat.

WEDDINGS AND WEDDING PREPARATIONS—Weddings do not take place on Shabbat. If unavoidable final preparations must be made on Shabbat for a Saturday evening wedding, care should be taken to preserve the spirit of Shabbat.

FUNERALS AND MOURNING—Funerals are not held on Shabbat, nor do people visit the cemetery. Although Shabbat does "count" as one of the days of *shivah*, mourners interrupt their mourning insofar as they do observe Shabbat at home and they do leave the house to attend synagogue services.

What other activities could I pursue on Shabbat afternoon?

STUDY A JEWISH TEXT—Over the centuries, part of Shabbat afternoon was customarily set aside for study. For example, during the summer after the festival of Shavuot, Pirkei Avot (Sayings of the Sages) was studied on Shabbat afternoon.

You and your family or a group of friends can continue in this tradition of textual study. Start with Pirkei Avot, selections from which are found in *Gates of Prayer,* or turn to the Torah portion of the week, which can be studied in *The Torah: A Modern Commentary*, published by the Union of American Hebrew Congregations. If you want to investigate other texts, your Rabbi can help you find appropriate materials.

SE-UDA SHELISHIT / THE THIRD MEAL OF SHABBAT—As was mentioned above, the rabbis of the Talmud mandated that the Jews of their time, who were used to eating only two meals a day, ought to distinguish Shabbat by making it a day on which they would eat three meals.

In the course of Jewish history the Friday evening and Shabbat noon meals were given special status that included the recitation of Kiddush. In contrast to this, the third meal was not associated with Kiddush. It developed into a simpler meal, somewhat of a snack, that was assigned to late afternoon on Shabbat. This simple meal was even given the straightforward name of Se-uda Shelishit, which translates literally as "third meal."

Approaching the end of Saturday afternoon, you may find Se-uda Shelishit to be a comfortable and relaxed way of concluding your Shabbat. Family and friends can come together for desserts or something light to eat. You can study together if you wish. After that, the group can bring Shabbat to a close with the service of Havdalah (page 62).

Separating from Shabbat
The Havdalah Service

Separating from Shabbat
The Havdalah Service

"Havdalah" means "separation." It refers to the beautiful and visual ceremony which ends Shabbat and thereby "separates" it from the weekdays.

The Havdalah service consists of:

1. Introduction
2. Blessing for wine
3. Blessing for spices
4. Blessing for light
5. Blessing of separation ("*havdalah*")
6. Conclusion

In order to conduct the Havdalah service, you will need a specially braided Havdalah candle, wine (if wine is unavailable, any beverage other than water may be used), and a spice box containing a variety of spices (for instance, cinnamon and cloves).

Everyone in the household should participate in Havdalah, although where children are present, the Havdalah candle is often held during the service by a child. It is customary to stand during Havdalah.

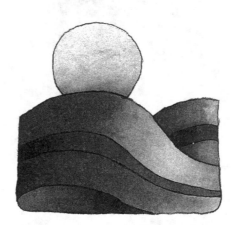

Havdalah

Introduction

As Shabbat ends, the Havdalah candle is kindled.
(You may read one of the following.)

If we take joy in the fullness of its spiritual pleasure, Shabbat is a taste of the messianic days. As Shabbat comes to an end and we confront darkness, we kindle light and speak words of confidence. We shall speak of *salvation*, deliverance from darkness; *salvation*, triumph of the work of redemption.

Legend tells us: As night descended at the end of the world's first Shabbat, Adam and Eve feared and wept. Then God showed them how to make fire and, by its light and warmth, to dispel the darkness and its terrors.

Kindling flame is a symbol of our first labor upon the earth. As Shabbat departs and the work week resumes, we kindle our own fire. We begin to separate ourselves from Shabbat by lighting the way into a new week with this candle.

(The following biblical verses may be read or chanted
along with the English version of the text. It is customary to lift the cup of wine
high when the last sentence in the Hebrew or English is read
and then proceed directly to the blessing for wine.)

Hi-nei Eil ye-shu-a-ti,	הִנֵּה אֵל יְשׁוּעָתִי,
ev-tach, ve-lo ef-chad.	אֶבְטַח וְלֹא אֶפְחָד.
Ki o-zi ve-zim-rat Ya A-do-nai,	כִּי עָזִּי וְזִמְרָת יָהּ יְיָ,
va-ye-hi li li-shu-a.	וַיְהִי־לִי לִישׁוּעָה.
U-she-av-tem ma-yim be-sa-son	וּשְׁאַבְתֶּם מַיִם בְּשָׂשׂוֹן
mi-ma-ai-nei ha-ye-shu-a.	מִמַּעַיְנֵי הַיְשׁוּעָה.
La-do-nai ha-ye-shu-a,	לַיְיָ הַיְשׁוּעָה,
al am-cha bir-cha-te-cha, se-la.	עַל־עַמְּךָ בִרְכָתֶךָ, סֶּלָה.

A-do-nai tse-va-ot i-ma-nu,
יְיָ צְבָאוֹת עִמָּנוּ,

mis-gav la-nu E-lo-hei Ya-a-kov,
מִשְׂגָּב־לָנוּ אֱלֹהֵי יַעֲקֹב,

se-la. A-do-nai tse-va-ot,
סֶלָה. יְיָ צְבָאוֹת,

ash-rei a-dam bo-tei-ach bach!
אַשְׁרֵי אָדָם בֹּטֵחַ בָּךְ!

A-do-nai, ho-shi-a;
יְיָ, הוֹשִׁיעָה;

ha-me-lech ya-a-nei-nu
הַמֶּלֶךְ יַעֲנֵנוּ

ve-yom kor-ei-nu.
בְיוֹם־קָרְאֵנוּ.

La-ye-hu-dim ha-ye-ta o-ra
לַיְהוּדִים הָיְתָה אוֹרָה

ve-sim-cha, ve-sa-son vi-kar;
וְשִׂמְחָה, וְשָׂשֹׂן וִיקָר;

kein ti-he-yeh la-nu.
כֵּן תִּהְיֶה לָנוּ.

Kos ye-shu-ot e-sa,
כּוֹס יְשׁוּעוֹת אֶשָּׂא,

u-ve-sheim A-do-nai e-ke-ra.
וּבְשֵׁם יְיָ אֶקְרָא.

God is my deliverance; I will be confident and unafraid. God is
my strength, my song and my salvation.
In joy we shall drink from the wells of salvation. God will rescue
and bless our people.
The God of all creation is with us; the God of Israel is our refuge.
Happy are those who trust in God.
The Jews had light, joy, delight, and honor; so may it be for us. I
lift up the cup of deliverance and call upon the Holy One.

Blessing for Wine   *The leader raises the cup of wine.*

Wine gladdens the heart. In our gladness, we see beyond the
injustice and violence which stain our world. Our eyes open to
unnoticed grace, blessings till now unseen, and the promise of
goodness we can bring to flower.

♪ See page 118

Ba-ruch a-ta, A-do-nai
בָּרוּךְ אַתָּה, יְיָ

E-lo-hei-nu, me-lech ha-o-lam,
אֱלֹהֵינוּ, מֶלֶךְ הָעוֹלָם,

bo-rei pe-ri ha-ga-fen.
בּוֹרֵא פְּרִי הַגָּפֶן.

We praise You, Adonai our God, Ruler of the universe, who
creates the fruit of the vine.

*(The leader does not drink the wine until after the final blessing
when Havdalah is fully complete.)*

Blessing for Spices

The leader holds up the spice box.

The added soul Shabbat confers is leaving now, and these spices will console us at the moment of its passing. They remind us that the six days will pass, and Shabbat return. Their scent makes us yearn for the sweetness of rest, and the dream of a world healed of pain, pure and wholesome as on the first Shabbat, when God, finding all things good, rested from the work of creation.

🎵 See page 118

Ba-ruch a-ta, A-do-nai

E-lo-hei-nu, me-lech ha-o-lam,

bo-rei mi-nei ve-sa-mim.

בָּרוּךְ אַתָּה, יְיָ

אֱלֹהֵינוּ, מֶלֶךְ הָעוֹלָם,

בּוֹרֵא מִינֵי בְשָׂמִים.

We praise You, Adonai our God, Ruler of the universe, who creates varieties of fragrant spices.

The leader shakes the spices, smells them, and passes them on so that everyone present may enjoy the fragrance.

Blessing for Light

Raise the Havdalah candle

The Havdalah candle is a unique candle. Its multiple wicks remind us that all qualities can be joined together. We have the power to create many different fires, some useful, others destructive. Let us be on guard never to let this gift of fire devour human life, sear cities and scorch fields, or foul the pure air we breathe. Let the fire we kindle be holy; let it bring light and warmth to all humanity.

🎵 See page 118

Ba-ruch a-ta, A-do-nai

E-lo-hei-nu, me-lech ha-o-lam,

bo-rei me-o-rei ha-eish.

בָּרוּךְ אַתָּה, יְיָ

אֱלֹהֵינוּ, מֶלֶךְ הָעוֹלָם,

בּוֹרֵא מְאוֹרֵי הָאֵשׁ.

We praise You, Adonai our God, Ruler of the universe, Creator of the lights of fire.

Cup the hands and extend them palms up toward the candle.

Blessing of Separation

Havdalah is not for the close of Shabbat alone;
    it is for all the days.
Havdalah means: separate yourself from the unholy;
    strive for holiness.
Havdalah means: separate yourself from fraud and exploitation,
    be fair and honest with all people.
Havdalah means: separate yourself from indifference to the poor
    and the deprived, the sick and the aged;
    work to ease their despair and their loneliness.
Havdalah means: separate yourself from hatred and violence;
    promote peace among people and nations.
May God give us understanding to reject the unholy and
    to choose the way of holiness.
May the One who separates the holy from the profane
    inspire us to perform these acts of Havdalah.

♪ See page 118

Ba-ruch a-ta, A-do-nai	בָּרוּךְ אַתָּה, יְיָ
E-lo-hei-nu, me-lech ha-o-lam,	אֱלֹהֵינוּ, מֶלֶךְ הָעוֹלָם,
ha-mav-dil bein ko-desh le-chol,	הַמַּבְדִּיל בֵּין קֹדֶשׁ לְחוֹל,
bein or le-cho-shech,	בֵּין אוֹר לְחְשֶׁךְ,
bein Yis-ra-eil la-a-mim,	בֵּין יִשְׂרָאֵל לָעַמִּים,
bein yom ha-she-vi-i	בֵּין יוֹם הַשְּׁבִיעִי
le-shei-shet ye-mei ha-ma-a-seh.	לְשֵׁשֶׁת יְמֵי הַמַּעֲשֶׂה.
Ba-ruch a-ta, A-do-nai,	בָּרוּךְ אַתָּה, יְיָ,
ha-mav-dil bein ko-desh le-chol.	הַמַּבְדִּיל בֵּין קֹדֶשׁ לְחוֹל.

We praise You, Adonai our God, who separates the holy from the
ordinary, light from darkness, who has called the people of Israel
to a destiny and purpose separate and distinct, and who separates
between the seventh day and the six weekdays. We praise You,
Adonai, who separates between the holy and the ordinary.

Sip the wine.

Conclusion

🎼 See page 119

*Extinguish the Havdalah candle in the remaining wine
while the following passages are sung or said.*

Ha-mav-dil bein ko-desh le-chol,	הַמַּבְדִּיל בֵּין קֹדֶשׁ לְחוֹל,
cha-to-tei-nu hu yim-chol,	חַטֹּאתֵינוּ הוּא יִמְחֹל,
zar-ei-nu ve-chas-pei-nu	זַרְעֵנוּ וְכַסְפֵּנוּ
yar-beh ka-chol,	יַרְבֶּה כַּחוֹל,
ve-cha-ko-cha-vim ba-lai-la.	וְכַכּוֹכָבִים בַּלָּיְלָה.

May God who separates the sacred from profane, forgive our sins and make us secure and as numerous as the sands on the shore of the sea and as the stars of night.

Sha-vu-a tov...	שָׁבוּעַ טוֹב...

A good week. A week of peace.
May gladness reign and joy increase.

❖

🎼 See page 120

Ei-li-ya-hu ha-na-vi,	אֵלִיָּהוּ הַנָּבִיא,
Ei-li-ya-hu ha-tish-bi;	אֵלִיָּהוּ הַתִּשְׁבִּי;
Ei-li-ya-hu, Ei-li-ya-hu,	אֵלִיָּהוּ, אֵלִיָּהוּ,
Ei-li-ya-hu ha-gil-a-di.	אֵלִיָּהוּ הַגִּלְעָדִי.
Bi-me-hei-ra ve-ya-mei-nu,	בִּמְהֵרָה בְיָמֵינוּ,
ya-vo ei-lei-nu;	יָבֹא אֵלֵינוּ;
im ma-shi-ach ben Da-vid,	עִם מָשִׁיחַ בֶּן דָּוִד,
im ma-shi-ach ben Da-vid.	עִם מָשִׁיחַ בֶּן דָּוִד.
Ei-li-ya-hu...	אֵלִיָּהוּ...

Elijah the prophet, Elijah the Tishbite. Elijah of Gilead. Soon, in our days, Elijah will come with the Messiah, the son of David.

What is the origin of Havdalah?

Havdalah is first mentioned in the Mishnah.[24] Looking back on such early rabbinic material, Maimonides explained the logic of Havdalah by referring to the rabbis' interpretation of the Shabbat commandment: "Remember the Sabbath day to keep it holy." (Exodus 20:8) According to Maimonides, the rabbis reasoned that "remembering" Shabbat required "sanctifying" Shabbat and that this ought to take place both as Shabbat arrived (with Friday evening Kiddush) and as it departed (with Saturday evening's Havdalah).[25]

When should Havdalah be said?

Just as most Reform Jews begin Shabbat when they start their Friday evening meal and light the candles, Reform Jews can also perform Havdalah in accordance with the rhythm of their own households. For some that will mean doing Havdalah after the sun has set and when three stars appear in the sky to signify that night has fully arrived.[26] Others may choose to do Havdalah toward the end of Saturday afternoon whenever the special activities they associate with Shabbat have come to an end.

What is the purpose of the introductory biblical verses in Havdalah?

The verses found at the beginning of Havdalah are taken from the biblical books of Isaiah, Psalms, and Esther. Each verse stresses the hope for deliverance or salvation, and in this way complements the traditional expectation that the Messiah will arrive for the redemption of the world right after Havdalah.

Even though one participant in the Havdalah service may begin the introductory verses on his or her own, it is customary for everyone present to join in saying the words from Esther 8:16, "The Jews had light, joy, delight, and honor." The group then continues with the wish—"So may it be for us."

Why is there a blessing for wine in this service?

To understand this practice, you need to recall the way in which wine is used on Friday evening. The goal at that time is to transform a weekday into the holy day of Shabbat, and wine is the vehicle by which a Jew accomplishes this process. That is why the Friday evening Kiddush contains two blessings: the longer one, which establishes that the seventh day is to be sanctified, plus the shorter one over the wine (...*borei peri hagafen*), which is necessary because consuming the wine is the act which actually initiates the sanctification of the day.

During Havdalah wine plays a similar role. It helps demarcate time—in this case the movement from the holy time of Shabbat back into the regular weekdays. As is the case on Friday evening, the wine blessing sets the stage for saying the blessing over the day (...*hamavdil bein kodesh lechol*). When that is done, the wine can be drunk, bringing the holy time of Shabbat to a close.

Why are there blessings for spices and light in this service?

Blessings for spices and light may be found in Havdalah to remind us of the ancient domestic custom of bringing spices on burning coals into the room at the end of a meal. Since the sages began their third Shabbat meal on Saturday afternoon, they would delay concluding the meal until Shabbat was over and the coals for heating the spices could be lit. The blessings then recited for the spices and the "light" (i.e., fire) that warmed them eventually became a part of Havdalah.

Another explanation for the use of spices:

Rabbinic legend offers an additional explanation for the use of spices. It suggests that, as a result of the peace and quiet of Shabbat, every Jew receives an additional soul (*neshama yeteira*). When this extra soul leaves at the end of Shabbat, the remaining soul of the Jew suffers a letdown. The smell of the spices at Havdalah is an attempt to buoy up the soul as it prepares for the coming week of work.[27]

Another explanation for use of light:

Rabbinic legend also offers several further explanations for the use of light at Havdalah. One source presents the blessing of light on Saturday night as a commemoration of what happened to Adam when it grew dark at the end of the first Shabbat. Because the first human being was afraid of the dark, God provided him with the knowledge to strike two stones together and create fire.[28] We remember the discovery of fire with the blessing of light at Havdalah.

Another text draws on the fact that, after Havdalah is said on Saturday, the first day of the next Jewish week begins. The text suggests that just as light was created on the first day of the first week in the Torah, a blessing for light ought to be included in Havdalah when the first day of all subsequent weeks arrives.[29]

Why is the Havdalah candle braided?

Since the blessing of light at Havdalah literally refers to God as "Creator of the lights of fire," the rabbis taught that the Havdalah candle should have at least two (if not more) wicks.[30] The result was the braided candle in today's Havdalah service. If such a candle is not available, two ordinary candles may be held together, so long as their separate wicks are brought together for one large flame.

Why do we look at our hands after the blessing for the light?

According to Jewish tradition, it is inappropriate to recite a blessing without following through on what you have blessed. In order to avoid such a blessing in vain (*beracha levatala*), it has become customary to "use" the light of the Havdalah candle after the blessing for light has been said. We accomplish this by extending our cupped hands toward the candle. The resulting interplay of light and shadow on our hands constitutes the "use" of the light.

How does the biblical prophet Elijah find his way into Havdalah?

Since Shabbat was understood to be a foretaste of the messianic era, over the centuries Jews have always hoped that Elijah, who was believed to be the forerunner of the Messiah, would arrive with the new week to announce the coming of a time that would be "all Shabbat."

Although Reform Jews have not literally subscribed to the notion of an individual Messiah descended from King David, the song "Eiliyahu Hanavi" (Elijah the Prophet) is still sung here and at the Pesach Seder to express the desire for an era when Elijah's passion for justice becomes a universal human commitment. For us, this would constitute the "coming of the Messiah."

Havdalah sounds wonderful. However, what if my observance of Shabbat is only partial? Is it hypocritical to do Havdalah if I haven't fully observed Shabbat up until this point?

No, it isn't. The premise of this guide is that the observance of Shabbat is not static. It changes and, hopefully, deepens for all Jews. Most importantly, every aspect of Shabbat is always available as an avenue for Jewish expression. For some readers of this guide, therefore, Havdalah may prove to be one of the most accessible aspects of Shabbat. Even though it comes at the end of Shabbat, Havdalah may commend itself because it so magnificently combines rituals that appeal to each of the senses while communicating the ultimate Jewish concern for wholeness and justice on our planet.

Readings and Meditations

Readings and Meditations

The prose and poetry in this section reflect some of the ways in which Shabbat has been understood over the span of Jewish history. The readings are assembled for purposes of study as well as the possibility of integrating some of them into your home observance.

From the Bible

The heaven and the earth were finished, and all their array. And on the seventh day God finished the work that had been done, and ceased on the seventh day from all the work that had been done. God blessed the seventh day and declared it holy, because on it God ceased from all the work of creation that had been done.

Genesis 2:1–3

Remember Shabbat and keep it holy. Six days you shall labor and do all your work, but the seventh day is a Sabbath of Adonai your God: you shall not do any work, you, your son or daughter, your male or female slave, or your cattle, or the stranger who is within your settlements. For in six days Adonai made heaven and earth and sea, and all that is in them, and rested on the seventh day; therefore Adonai blessed Shabbat and sanctified it.

Exodus 20:8–11

The people of Israel shall keep Shabbat, observing Shabbat throughout the generations as a covenant for all time. It shall be a sign for ever between Me and the people of Israel, for in six days God made heaven and earth, and on the seventh day God rested and was refreshed.

Exodus 31:16–17

Observe Shabbat and keep it holy, as Adonai your God has commanded you. Six days you shall labor and do all your work but the seventh day is a sabbath of Adonai your God: you shall not do any work, you, your son or your daughter, your male or female slave, your ox or your ass, or any of your cattle, or the stranger in your settlements, so that your male and female slave may rest as you do. Remember that you were a slave in the land of Egypt and Adonai your God freed you from there with a mighty hand and an outstretched arm; therefore Adonai your God has commanded you to observe Shabbat.

Deuteronomy 5:12–15

If you refrain from trampling Shabbat,
From pursuing your business on My holy day;
And call Shabbat a joy,
And the holy day of Adonai honorable;
And if you will honor it without doing what you always do,
Not pursuing your business, nor even speaking of it;
Then shall you delight yourself in Adonai,
And I will make you to ride upon the high places of the earth,
And I will nourish you with the heritage of Jacob your father,
For the mouth of Adonai has spoken it.

Isaiah 58:13–14

(To be said to a man at the Erev Shabbat meal)

Blessed is the man who reveres Adonai,
who greatly delights in God's commandments.
His descendants will be honored in the land:
the generation of the upright will be blessed.
His household prospers,
and his righteousness endures for ever.
Light shines in the darkness for the upright;
for the one who is gracious, compassionate, and just.
He is not afraid of evil tidings;
his mind is firm, trusting in Adonai.
His heart is steady, he will not be afraid.
He gives freely to the poor;
his righteousness endures for ever; his life is exalted in honor.

From Psalm 112

(To be said to a woman at the Erev Shabbat meal)

A woman of valor—who can find?
For she is to be valued above rubies.
Her husband trusts in her, and so he lacks nothing.
She does him good, never harm, all the days of her life.
She reaches out to those in need, and extends her hands
    to the poor.
She is clothed in strength and dignity, and she faces the future
    cheerfully.
She speaks with wisdom; the law of kindness is on her lips.
Her children rise up and bless her; her husband sings
    her praises.
Many daughters have done valiantly, but you excel them all.

From Proverbs 31

From Rabbinic Literature

When the world was created, Shabbat said to the Holy One, "Ruler of the Universe, every living thing created has its mate, and each day has its companion, except me, the seventh day. I am alone!" God answered, "The people of Israel will be your mate."

When the Israelites arrived at Mount Sinai, the Holy One said to them, "Remember what I said to Shabbat—that the people of Israel would be her mate?" It is with reference to this that My fourth commandment for you reads: "*Remember* the Sabbath day, to keep it holy."

Genesis Rabbah 11:8

Once the Torah asked, "God of the world, when the people Israel enters the Promised Land, what will become of me? Each Israelite will be busy with plowing and sowing his field, and what, then, will happen to me?" God answered the Torah, "I have a love partner which I am giving to You. It is Shabbat. When Israel ceases working, they will enter synagogues and study places and devote themselves to working with Torah."

Sefer Ha-Agadah 381:22

The main categories of work are forty save one: sowing, ploughing, reaping, binding sheaves, threshing, winnowing, cleansing crops, grinding, sifting, kneading, baking, shearing wool, washing or beating or dyeing it, spinning, weaving, making two loops, weaving two threads, separating two threads, tying [a knot], loosening [a knot], sewing two stitches, tearing in order to sew two stitches, hunting a gazelle, slaughtering or flaying or salting it or curing its skin, scraping it or cutting it up, writing two letters, erasing in order to write two letters, building, pulling down, putting out a fire, lighting a fire, striking with a hammer and taking anything from one domain into another. These are the main categories of work: forty save one.

Mishnah *Shabbat* 7:2

God said to the people of Israel: "If you observe My commandments I will give you My most precious gift." Israel asked: "What will that be?" God said: "The future world."

Alphabet of Rabbi Akiba

How do we know that the duty of saving life supersedes Shabbat? Rabbi Yochanan ben Joseph said, "It is written in the Torah 'You shall keep Shabbat, for it is holy *unto you*.' [Exodus 31:14]. This implies that Shabbat is committed to you, not you to Shabbat."

Talmud *Yoma* 85b

The laws of the Shabbat are set aside in cases where there is danger to life, as is the case with all the mitzvot. Therefore, a sick person who is in danger may have all his needs taken care of on the Shabbat (even when so doing violates the laws of Shabbat) if it is so ordered by a doctor. If there is some question as to the seriousness of the illness (as in the case where one doctor says there is danger and another says there is not), then the Shabbat is set aside on the principle that, when there is any doubt about danger to life, we set aside the Shabbat in order to save life.

Maimonides,
Mishneh Torah *Hilchot Shabbat* 11:5

From Modern Sources

The pauses between the notes

A great pianist was once asked by an ardent admirer: "How do you handle the notes as well as you do?" The artist answered: "The notes I handle no better than many pianists, but the pauses between the notes—ah! that is where the art resides."

In great living, as in great music, the art may be in the pauses. Surely one of the enduring contributions which Judaism made to the art of living was the Shabbat, "the pause between the notes." And it is to the Shabbat that we must look if we are to restore to our lives the sense of serenity and sanctity which Shabbat offers in such joyous abundance.

Likrat Shabbat

On the meaning of Shabbat

Six days a week we humans use time. We value it as a means to an end. Time "well spent" for us is time that helps us acquire something.

Yet to have more does not mean to be more. Indeed, there is a realm of time where the goal is not to have, but to be, not to own, but to give, not to control, but to share, not to subdue, but to be in accord. Life goes wrong when the control of space, the acquisition of things, becomes our sole concern.

The seventh day rights our balance and restores our perspective. It is like a palace in time with a kingdom for all. It is not a date, but an atmosphere.

On the seventh day, we celebrate time rather than space. Six days we live under the tyranny of things of space; on the seventh day we try to become attuned to holiness in time.

It is a day on which we are called upon to share in what is eternal in time. To turn from the results of creation to the mystery of creation; from the world of creation to the creation of the world.

Adapted from Abraham Joshua Heschel

Tension and psychic stress

By and large we modern Jews are not exhausted by physical exertions during our work week. Few of us dig tunnels, unload cargoes, mine coal, man steel furnaces, or operate heavy machinery. We do not go to work by trudging many miles on foot. We have at our disposal the amenities of the automobile, caught in traffic jams, or commuter trains invariably crowded and late, or the buses and subways, of which the less said the better. By the end of the week our muscles are not physically fatigued; instead, our nerves are frayed. Not toil, but tension, is the toll that modern life exacts from us and from our contemporaries. We need rest and surcease, not so much from physical strain as from psychic stress built up during the week.

It is precisely the traditional Sabbath that speaks to our present condition, by enjoining the avoidance of travel, shopping, cooking, and writing, and by limiting our movements to what we can do with our own power, by walking. What the prayer book beautifully describes as *menucha shelema*, "total rest," is only within the power of the traditional Sabbath to bestow. As tensions continue to mount in contemporary society, the traditional Sabbath, that requires an all-but-total separation from work-a-day tasks and concerns and worry, becomes an ever more precious resource for life in a world increasingly dedicated to death.

Robert Gordis

A traditional perspective on Shabbat as a day for restoring the world to God

How, above all, do we show our domination over the earth? In that we can fashion all things in our environment to our own purpose—the earth for our habitation and source of sustenance; plant and animal for food and clothing. We can transform everything into an instrument of human service. We are allowed to rule over the world for six days with God's will. On the seventh day, however, we are forbidden by divine behest to fashion anything for our purpose. In this way we acknowledge that we have no rights of ownership or authority over the world. Nothing may be dealt with as we please, for everything belongs to God, the Creator, who has set human beings into the world to rule it according to the divine word. On each Sabbath day, the world, so to speak, is restored to God, and thus we proclaim, both to ourselves and to our surroundings, that we enjoy only a borrowed authority.

Adapted from Samson Raphael Hirsch

An explanation of the traditional definition for work

The concept of work is not one of physical effort. Work is any interference, be it constructive or destructive, with the physical world. Rest is a state of peace between humanity and nature. We must leave nature untouched, not change it in any way, either by building or by destroying anything. Even the smallest change we make in the natural process is a violation of rest. The Sabbath is the day of complete harmony between humanity and nature. Work is any kind of disturbance of the humanity-nature equibililbrium.

Any heavy work, like plowing or building, is work in this, as well as our modern, sense. But lighting a match and pulling up a blade of grass, while not requiring any effort, are symbols of human interference with the natural process. As such, they are also a breach of peace between human beings and nature.

On the basis of this principle, we can understand the talmudic prohibition of carrying anything, even of little weight, on one's person. In fact, the carrying of something, as such, is not forbidden. I can carry a heavy load within my house or my estate without violating the Sabbath law. But I must not carry even a handkerchief from one domain to another—for instance, from the private domain of the house to the public domain of the street. This law is an extension of the idea of peace from the social to the natural realm. A person must not interfere with or change the natural equilibrium and must also refrain from changing the social equilibrium. That means not only not to do business but also to avoid the most primitive form of transference of property, namely, its local transference from one domain to another.

The Sabbath symbolizes a state of union between humanity and nature and between one human being and another. By not working—that is to say, by not participating in the process of natural and social change—we are free from the chains of time.

Rest in the sense of the traditional Sabbath concept is quite different from rest being defined as not working, or not making an effort (just as "peace"— shalom—in the prophetic tradition is more than merely the absence of war; it expresses harmony, wholeness).

Adapted from Erich Fromm

Modern Poetry and Prayer

Sabbath Prayer

God, help us now to make this new Shabbat.
After noise, we seek quiet;
After crowds of indifferent strangers,
We seek to touch those we love;
After concentration on work and responsibility,
We seek freedom to meditate, to listen to our inward selves.
We open our eyes to the hidden beauties
and the infinite possibilities in the world You are creating;
We break open the gates of the reservoirs
of goodness and kindness in ourselves and in others;
We reach toward one holy perfect moment of Shabbat.

Ruth Brin

Light a Candle

Light a candle.
Drink wine.
Softly the Sabbath has plucked
the sinking sun.
Slowly the Sabbath descends,
the rose of heaven in her hand.

How can the Sabbath
plant a huge and shining flower
in a blind and narrow heart?
How can the Sabbath
plant the bud of angels
in a heart of raving flesh?
Can the rose of eternity grow
in an age enslaved
to destruction,
an age enslaved
to death?

Light a candle!
Drink wine!
Slowly the Sabbath descends
and in her hand
the flower, and in her hand the sinking sun.

Zelda

Out of the Land of Heaven

Out of the land of heaven
Down comes the warm Sabbath sun
Into the spice-box of earth
The Queen will make every Jew her lover.
    In a white silk coat
Our rabbi dances up the street,
Wearing our lawns like a green prayer-shawl,
Brandishing houses like silver flags.
    Behind him dance his pupils,
Dancing not so high
And chanting the rabbi's prayer,
But not so sweet.
    And who waits for him
On a throne at the end of the street
But the Sabbath Queen.
    Down go his hands
Into the spice-box of earth,
And there he finds the fragrant sun
For a wedding ring,
And draws her wedding finger through.
    Now back down the street they go,
Dancing higher than the silver flags.
His pupils somewhere have found wives too,
And all are chanting the rabbi's song
And leaping high in the perfumed air.
    Who calls him Rabbi?
Cart-horse and dogs call him Rabbi,
And he tells them:
The Queen makes every Jew her lover
And gathering on their green lawns
The people call him Rabbi,
And fill their mouths with good bread
And his happy song.

Leonard Cohen

Erev Shabbas

It's so stupid.
Wednesday afternoon,
soaked in the idiotica of errands
and all those "things to do"
that steal a man's minutes, his years —
I forgot the Queen.
Her Majesty was due at four-eighteen
on Friday, not a minute later,
and I was wasting hands, words, steps,
racing to a rushing finish-line
of roaring insignificance
I just as well could fill
with preparations for the royal entourage:
cleaning and cleansing each act's doing,
each word's saying,
in anticipation of the Great Event of Shabbas.

Who am I that she should wish
to spend the day with me?
I dry out my strengths, cook, move dust,
casually insensitive to all the songs
reminding me that she, the Queen,
in diamond-ruby-emerald-glow tiara,
would come to grace my table.
She comes,
no matter how the week was spent,
in joy or in silliness,
yet she comes.
And I am her host,
laying a linen flower tablecloth
that is white,
that is all the colors of the rainbow.

This is the Jews' sense of royalty;
she never does not spend one day a week
with me, and every Jew,
in the open air of freedom,
or lightening the misery of prisoners
in stinking Russian prisons
or the ghettoes of Damascus.

Come, my Shabbas Queen,
embodiment of Worlds-to-Be:
Your gracious kindness is our breath of life,
and though we once, twice, all-too-often
fail to say, "How beautiful your cape!
How lovely your hair, your Shechina-eyes!"
we will not always be so lax,
apathetic to your grace, your presence.
Touch us again this week
with your most unique love's tenderness,
and we shall sing to you our songs,
dance our dances in your honor,
and sigh for you our sighs
of longing, peace, and hope.

Danny Siegel

A Blessing for the Family

We thank You, O God, for our family and for what we mean and bring to one another. We are grateful for the bonds of loyalty and affection which sustain us and for the capacity to love and to care.

Help us to be modest in our demands of one another, but generous in our giving to each other. May we never measure how much love or encouragement we offer; may we never count the times we forgive. Rather, may we always be grateful that we have one another and that we are able to express our love in acts of kindness.

Keep us gentle in our speech. When we offer words of criticism, may they be chosen with care and spoken softly. May we waste no opportunity to speak words of sympathy, of appreciation, of praise.

Bless our family with health, happiness, and contentment. Above all, grant us the wisdom to build a joyous and peaceful home in which Your spirit will always abide. Amen.

Slow Me Down, God

Slow me down, God!
Ease the pounding of my heart, by the quieting of my mind.
Steady my hurried pace with the vision of the eternal reach
    of time.
Give me, amidst the confusion of my day, the calmness
    of the everlasting hills.

Break the tensions of my nerves and muscles with the soothing
    music of the singing streams that live in my memory.
Help me to know the magical restoring power of sleep.
Teach me the art of taking a minute's vacation—of slowing down
    to look at a flower, to chat with a friend, to pat a dog,
    to read a few lines from a good book.
Remind me each day of the fable of the hare and the tortoise,
    that I may know that the race is not always to the swift,
    that there is more to life than increasing its speed.
Let me look upward into the branches of the towering oak tree
    and know that it grew great and strong
    because it grew slowly and well.
Slow me down, God, and inspire me to send my roots deep into
    the soil of life's enduring values that I may grow toward
    the stars of greater destiny.

               Adapted from Wilfred A. Peterson

I Have Plenty of Time

I went out, God.
People were coming and going, walking and running.
Everything was rushing: cars, trucks, the street, the whole town.
People were rushing not to waste time.
They were rushing after time,
To catch up with time, to gain time.
Good-bye sir, excuse me, I haven't time.
I'll come back, I can't wait, I haven't time.
I must end this letter—I haven't time.
I'd love to help you, but I haven't time.
I can't accept, having no time.
I can't think, I can't read, I'm swamped, I haven't time.
I'd like to pray, but I haven't time.
You understand, God, they simply haven't the time.
The child is playing, he hasn't time right now…later on…
The young married has his house, he has to fix it up.
    He hasn't time…later on…
They are dying. Too late! They have no more time!

And so all people run after time, God.
They pass through life running, hurried, jostled, overburdened,
     frantic, and they never get there.
They still haven't time.
In spite of all their efforts, they're still short of time.
Of a great deal of time.

God, You must have made a mistake in Your calculations.
The hours are too short, the days are too short,
     our lives are too short.
You who are beyond time, God, You smile to see us fighting it.
And You know what You are doing.
You make no mistakes in Your distributions of time to people.
You give each one time to do what You want him to do.
But we must not deface time,
     waste time
     kill time,
For time is not only a gift that You give us
But a perishable gift,
A gift that does not keep.

God, I have time.
I have plenty of time,
All the time You gave me.
The years of my life,
The days of my years,
The hours of my days,
They are all mine,
Mine to fill quietly, calmly
But to fill completely to the brim.

                                        Michael Quoist

Where Has This Week Vanished?

Where has this week vanished?
Is it lost for ever?
Will I ever recover anything from it?
The joy of life, the unexpected victory,
the realized hope, the task accomplished?
Will I ever be able to banish the memory of pain,
the sting of defeat, the heaviness of boredom?
On this day let me keep for a while what must drift away.
On this day let me be free of the burdens that must return.
On this day, Shabbat, abide.

And now Shabbat has come,
can it help me to withdraw for a while
from the flight of time?
Can it contain the retreat of the hours and days from the
grasp of a frantic life?
When all days abandon me, Shabbat, abide.

Let me learn to pause, if only for this day.
Let me find peace on this day.
Let me enter into a quiet world this day.
On this day, Shabbat, abide.

David Polish

The Need to Pray

To pray is so necessary and so hard. Hard not because it requires intellect or knowledge or a big vocabulary, but because it requires of us humility. And that comes, I think, from a profound sense of one's brokenness, and one's need. Not the need that causes us to cry, "Get me out of this trouble, quick!" but the need that one feels every day of one's life—even though one does not acknowledge it—to be related to something bigger than one's self, something more alive than one's self, something older and something not yet born, that will endure through time.

Lillian Smith

Sensing the Miracles in Our World

The sense for the "miracles which are daily with us," the sense for the "continual marvels," is the source of prayer. There is no worship, no music, no love, if we take for granted the blessings or defeats of living. No routine of the social, physical, or physiological order must dull our sense of surprise at the fact that there *is* a social, a physical, or a physiological order. We are trained in maintaining our sense of wonder by uttering a prayer....To pray is to take notice of the wonder, to regain a sense of the mystery that animates all beings, the divine margin in all attainments.

Abraham Joshua Heschel

Glory Be to You for Chance Encounters

Glory be to You for chance encounters.

All praise to You,
for You occasion momentary Torah
in incidental happenings:
Shabbas strollers' eyes, conductors' hands,
the jumping feet of children.

You set us unexpected meetings everywhere
in corridors and clinics, waiting rooms, the beach.

You make signs and signals
radiating warmth
in everything
if we but look for them.
Boredom is a sin.

For as long as there are
trees and mountains (traces of Design),
lakes and wrinkled faces
moving towards us
in a patterned unpredictability
we say:
Glory to You, Lord;
accept our Psalms of praise.

Danny Siegel

For the Blessings

For the blessings which You lavish upon us
in forest and sea, in mountain and meadow, in rain and sun,
we thank You.

For the blessings You implant within us,
joy and peace, meditation and laughter,
we are grateful to You.

For the blessings of friendship and love,
of family and community,

For the blessings we ask of You
and those we cannot ask,

For the blessings You bestow upon us openly
and those You give us in secret,

For all these blessings,
we thank You and are grateful to You.

For the blessings we recognize
and those we fail to recognize,

For the blessings of our tradition
and of our holy days,

For the blessings of return and forgiveness,
of memory, of vision, and of hope—

For all these blessings which surround us on every side
Dear God, hear our thanks and accept our gratitude.

Ruth Brin

The Thread

Something is very gently,
invisibly, silently,
pulling at me—a thread
or net of threads
finer than cobweb and as
elastic. I haven't tried
the strength of it. No barbed
hook pierced and tore me.
Was it not long ago this
thread began to draw me?
Or way back? Was I
born with its knot about my
neck, a bridle? Not fear
but a stirring
of wonder makes me
catch my breath when I feel
the tug of it when I thought
it had loosened itself and gone.

Denise Levertov

One

In the beginning, way on high,
the light was One,
yet descending it parted
to become
the blessing in the corn
in the flower the lace,
a gleam in the eye
and a smile
on the face,
in the muscles strong
and in the soul—a song.

Yet when
the grain be threshed
and the sapling crushed,
when
the eye shall dim
and the smile shall fade
and the vigor wilt
and the song be stilled,
and all the rivers to their source
have run—
the light
on that day
shall again
be—One.

Tzvi Ya'ir

Taking the Next Step

Thinking in Terms of Mitzvah/Commandment for Reform Jews

Just as the various aspects of Shabbat have their own background, this guidebook for Shabbat also has a history. It follows the publication of two other volumes by the Reform rabbinate, each of which also stressed the significance of Jewish practice. The first, *Shaarei Mitzvah/Gates of Mitzvah*, presented the life cycle; the second, *Shaarei Mo-eid/Gates of the Seasons*, took up the subject of observing the Jewish holidays.

All three of these books were preceded in 1972 by the text on which this volume is modeled, *A Shabbat Manual*. That book was edited by Rabbi W. Gunther Plaut and was noteworthy because it was the first publication of the Central Conference of American Rabbis devoted to the observance of Shabbat in terms of mitzvah/commandment.

Such an approach toward Jewish practice was novel and even controversial at the time because Reform Judaism has always allowed individual Jews freedom in shaping their own Jewish lives. The *Shabbat Manual* maintained, however, that in addition to the need for autonomy in Jewish decision-making, there also ought to be some sense of discipline among Reform Jews.

The concern was that without some counterbalance to the autonomy of the individual, Reform Judaism could be fragmented into as many divisions as there were individual Jews. Each Jew could make Shabbat as he or she wished without any sense of commonality or even minimum observance. "Mitzvah" was the word used in the *Shabbat Manual* to signal that Reform Jews needed to reassess their attitudes toward radical freedom in the area of Jewish practice. By using the word "mitzvah," the *Shabbat Manual* asked Reform Jews to begin thinking about their Jewish observances in terms of commandment or obligation.

Rabbi Plaut wrote, "Mitzvah is what a Jew ought to do in response to God and to the tradition of our people." The *Shabbat Manual* listed a full regimen of Shabbat observances, calling them mitzvot, and Rabbi Plaut commented, "It is suggested that you make a permanent decision to apply the principles of this catalogue of mitzvot to your life. You may do this for yourself alone, or together with your family, or as a member of a group of like-minded Jews who seek such a commitment."

Shabbat Becomes a Mitzvah

Almost two decades later the invitation to observe Shabbat remains a challenge for Reform Jews. That is why this book was created. It was designed to allow Reform Jews the fullest opportunity to ask questions, explore Shabbat, and find a path through "the gates of Shabbat." The hope was that if Reform Jews had a text which helped them encounter the beauty and joy of Shabbat, they would embrace Shabbat as a necessity in their lives. In other words, *Shabbat would become a mitzvah for Reform Jews.*

When all is said and done, the commitment to Shabbat which raises it to the level of a mitzvah may not yet be what you feel. If you have just begun to discover Shabbat, that is not surprising. You are probably still trying to integrate the many facets of Shabbat into your life, and that process takes time and patience.

On the other hand, even those who are accustomed to Shabbat may not find it easy to use the term mitzvah/commandment when it comes to describing their practice. As moderns, most of us are very hesitant when it comes to accepting any notion of external authority or regimen.

Nevertheless, Jews have used the term mitzvah/commandment for centuries in describing the obligation they felt to live their lives Jewishly. Jews have followed mitzvot not solely out of compulsion but because living Jewishly provided an inner source of fulfillment and joy.

In regard to Shabbat, this guide attempts to communicate these positive feelings of satisfaction and pride. Hopefully, your experience of Shabbat will add a dimension of sanctity to your life that nothing else can replace. When that happens, *you ought to begin to feel commanded to observe Shabbat because you would not want to do anything but that.* At that time what you do will not only strengthen you as a Jew, but also strengthen the Jewish people.

We now turn to two brief discussions of mitzvot followed by a recapitulation of all the possibilities for Shabbat described in this guide. This time around, the possibilities of Shabbat are presented in terms of mitzvah. Our goal is to communicate the belief that being a Jew has to mean at least the attempt to make Shabbat a part of our lives.

The Meaning of Mitzvah

Mitzvah (plural, *mitzvot*) is what a Jew ought to do in response to God and to the tradition of our people. This response comes from personal commitment rather than from unquestioning obedience to a set of commandments which past tradition thought to be the direct will of God. By making choice and commitment part of our plan of life, we willingly and purposefully strengthen our bonds with the God of Israel and with our people.

Mitzvah is, therefore, more than folkway and ceremony. As we choose to do a mitzvah — be it a positive act or a negative act (an abstention) — we choose the way of duty, of self-discipline, and of loyalty. To do so with eagerness and joy is the true seal of Shabbat observance.

This manual lists Shabbat mitzvot and offers options and opportunities. It is suggested that you make a permanent decision to apply the principles of this catalogue of mitzvot to your life. You may do this for yourself alone, or together with your family, or a member of a group of like-minded Jews who seek such a commitment....

How much ought I observe? To make Shabbat meaningful, observe as much as you can. Begin from where you are now, with what you presently do or do not do. If your Shabbat is like a weekday, begin with any mitzvah, but begin. Make your decision into a habit. From a modest start you may progress to a more significant observance. If you presently observe some mitzvot, search for the opportunity to deepen or enlarge that practice.

You must always remember that you are performing mitzvot. It is not a question of "how you feel about it" at any given time. You may not be "in the mood." But being a Jew is not always convenient or easy. The performance of mitzvot ought to be the pattern of one's life. The more deep-rooted such a pattern, the more intense and regular one's performance of mitzvot, the richer and truer will be one's life as a Jew. Do not become discouraged because the manual contains mitzvot which you cannot now fulfill. The secret of observing a mitzvah is to begin.

W. Gunther Plaut
From *A Shabbat Manual*

Mitzvah is the key to authentic Jewish existence and to the sanctification of life. No English equivalent can adequately translate the term. Its root meaning is "commandment," but mitzvah has come to have broader meaning. It suggests the joy of doing something for the sake of others and for the sake of God, and it conveys still more: it also speaks of living Jewishly, of meeting life's challenges and opportunities in particular ways. All this is mitzvah. Doing one mitzvah, says our tradition, will lead us to do another and another.

This book was written by Reform rabbis. Reform Judaism attempts responses to the conditions of each age in order to make it possible for Jews to live their Judaism meaningfully and richly. Such Jewish responses should seek to preserve the continuity of Jewish life and at the same time be sensitive to opportunities for desirable innovation.

In an earlier stage, Reform sought to distinguish between ethical and ritual mitzvot. It was argued that the ethical commandments were valid eternally and thus binding upon Jews of every generation. The ritual commandments, however, were considered linked to particular experiences or circumstances, and therefore they were considered optional or even superfluous. But this dichotomy is often arbitrary, for ethical resolve and ritual expression, intention and act, are in fact closely interlinked, as are reason and feeling. Ritual, as the vehicle for confronting God and Jewish history, can shape and stimulate one's ethical impulses. Therefore, the ancient advice is still valid: the very act of doing a mitzvah may lead one to know the heart of the matter.

This book was conceived to help Jews make Jewish responses, to give their lives Jewish depth and character. It recognizes that not all Jews need to do the same thing or make the same responses, that even within the realm of each mitzvah various levels of doing or understanding might exist. Reform Judaism maintains the principle of individual freedom; each Jew must make a personal decision about the Judaism which has come down through the ages.

Nevertheless, all Jews who acknowledge themselves to be members of their people and its tradition thereby limit their freedom to some extent. This book is an expression of Reform Jewish philosophy in that it is built on the twin commitments which each Jew ought to have, the commitments to Jewish continuity and to personal freedom of choice.

Simeon J. Maslin
From the Introduction to *Shaarei Mitzvah/Gates of Mitzvah*

The Mitzvot of Shabbat:
An Overview of Shabbat Observance

This summary of Shabbat observance was adapted from *Shaarei Mo-eid/Gates of the Seasons*, which based its own listing of the Shabbat mitzvot on an original presentation of the mitzvot in *A Shabbat Manual*. Extensive footnotes are available in *Shaarei Mo-eid* (see "Further Reading," page 103).

The mitzvah of Shabbat observance

It is a mitzvah for every Jew, single or married, young or old, to observe Shabbat. The unique status of Shabbat is demonstrated by its being the only one of the holy days to be mentioned in the Ten Commandments. Its observance distinguishes the Jewish people as a Covenant People.

> The people of Israel shall keep Shabbat, observing Shabbat throughout the generations as a covenant for all time. It shall be a sign for ever between Me and the people of Israel.
>
> (Exodus 31:16–17)

Shabbat observance involves both positive and negative mitzvot, i.e., doing and refraining from doing.

The mitzvah of oneg/joy

It is a mitzvah to take delight in Shabbat observance, as Isaiah said, "You shall call Shabbat a delight" (58:13). Oneg implies celebration and relaxation, sharing time with loved ones, enjoying the beauty of nature, eating a leisurely meal made special with conviviality and song, visiting with friends and relatives, taking a leisurely stroll, reading, and listening to music. All of these are appropriate expressions of oneg. Because of the special emphasis on oneg, Jewish tradition recommended sexual relations between husband and wife on Shabbat.[31]

The mitzvah of kedushah/holiness

It is a mitzvah to sanctify Shabbat by setting it apart from the other days of the week. The Torah depicts Shabbat as the culmination of Creation and describes God as blessing it and sanctifying it (making it *Shabbat Kodesh*). Every Jew should partake of this day's special nature and abstain from that which lessens his or her awareness of its distinctive character. Shabbat must be distinguished from the other days of the week so that those who observe it may be transformed by its kedushah/holiness.

The mitzvah of menucha/rest

It is a mitzvah to rest on Shabbat. However, Shabbat menucha/rest implies much more than simply refraining from work. The concept of Shabbat rest includes both physical relaxation (for example, a Shabbat afternoon nap) and tranquillity of mind and spirit. On Shabbat one deliberately turns away from weekday pressures and activities. The pace of life on Shabbat should be different from that of the rest of the week.

Conversations should not focus on the problems of everyday existence but rather on the meaning of life and the awareness of beauty in God's creation. One might choose, for example, to walk more slowly on Shabbat in order to absorb one's surroundings and to enjoy the relaxed atmosphere of Shabbat.

If the week is characterized by competition, rush, and turmoil, their absence will contribute to serenity and to the rejuvenation of body and spirit. It is this unique quality of menucha which moves our tradition to call Shabbat "a foretaste of the days of the Messiah."[32]

The mitzvah of refraining from work

It is a mitzvah to refrain from work on Shabbat, as it is said: "Six days you shall labor and do all your work, but the seventh day is a Sabbath of Adonai your God; you shall not do any work" (Exodus 20:9–10). Abstinence from work is a major expression of Shabbat observance;* however, it is no simple matter to define work today. Certain activities which some do to earn a living, others do for relaxation or to express their creativity. Clearly, though, one should avoid one's normal occupation or profession on Shabbat whenever possible and engage only in those types of activities which enhance the oneg/joy, menucha/rest, and kedusha/holiness of the day.

Social events during Shabbat worship hours

It is inappropriate to schedule social events at a time that conflicts with the Shabbat worship hours set by the congregation, and thereby to cause friends and relatives to choose between joining the congregation in worship or attending the event. One should not attend social events scheduled for these hours. Jewish organizations should be particularly careful in this matter.

---

* Where circumstances require an individual to perform work on the Shabbat, that individual should nevertheless bear in mind that refraining from work is a major goal of Shabbat observance and he/she should perform as many Shabbat mitzvot as possible.

Public events on Shabbat

The scheduling of, or participation in, public events on Shabbat violates the sanctity of Shabbat. Therefore, it may become necessary to object to civic functions on Shabbat, especially those conflicting with Shabbat worship hours, and to refuse to participate in them.

The mitzvah of preparation

It is a mitzvah to prepare for Shabbat. According to the Rabbis, this mitzvah is implied in the Exodus version of the Ten Commandments, "Remember Shabbat and keep it holy" (Exodus 20:8). Preparations may begin well before Shabbat by buying special food or waiting to wear a new garment for Shabbat. Wherever possible, all members of the household should be involved in Shabbat preparations.

The mitzvah of hachnasat orchim / hospitality

It is a mitzvah to invite guests to join in the celebration of Shabbat. Ideally, no one should have to observe Shabbat alone. Therefore, one should pay particular attention to newcomers in the community and others who are alone. Although every Jew is obligated to celebrate Shabbat whether at home or away, the joy of Shabbat is increased by joining with others. The mitzvah is called *hachnasat orchim.*

The mitzvah of tzedakah

It is always a mitzvah to give tzedakah. Following the example of talmudic sages, the tradition has recognized the final moments before Shabbat as one of the regular opportunities to perform the mitzvah. The placing of money in a tzedakah box just prior to lighting the Shabbat candles is an excellent way to observe this mitzvah and to teach it to children.

The mitzvah of Hadlakat Neirot / Shabbat Candlelighting

It is a mitzvah to begin the observance of Shabbat with the kindling of Shabbat candles followed by the recitation of the appropriate blessing.

The lighting of candles in the synagogue is not a substitute for performance of the mitzvah in the home.

The mitzvah of Kiddush

It is a mitzvah to recite Kiddush over wine at the Shabbat table. The recitation of Kiddush in the synagogue is not a substitute for the performance of the mitzvah in the home.

The mitzvah of blessing children

It is a mitzvah for a parent or parents to bless child(ren) at the Shabbat table each week.

The mitzvah of the Motsi

It is a mitzvah to recite the Motsi at every meal. On Shabbat, it is recited over challah, which is either cut or broken and then eaten by all present.

The Shabbat table

The mitzvah of taking delight in Shabbat is appropriately expressed at the Shabbat meal. Special foods and beverages should grace the table. Joy is enhanced by singing Shabbat zemirot/songs.

The mitzvah of Birkat Hamazon

At the conclusion of all meals, and of course on Shabbat, it is a mitzvah to recite grace after meals (Birkat Hamazon).

The mitzvah of congregational worship

It is a mitzvah to join the congregation in worship on Shabbat.

The Shabbat noon meal

The noon meal provides additional opportunities for making Shabbat special. The mitzvot of Kiddush, Motsi, and Birkat Hamazon should be observed, as well as the singing of zemirot, as on Friday evening.

The mitzvah of talmud torah / study

It is a mitzvah to study Torah every day, even more so on Shabbat. The reading of the *sidra*, the weekly Torah portion, during the synagogue service should lead to further appropriate reading and related study.

The mitzvah of bikur cholim / visiting the sick

It is a mitzvah to visit the ill and shut-ins at any time. The Talmud, elaborating on the Mishnah,[33] lists visiting the sick as one of the ten basic mitzvot for which "a person is rewarded in this world and the world to come." By performing this mitzvah on Shabbat, one brings the sick a measure of Shabbat joy.

Berit mila / the covenant of circumcision

The Torah is very clear about the importance and the timing of circumcision for a male child: "Throughout the generations, every male among you shall be circumcised at the age of eight days." (Genesis 17:12)

Because of this verse, Jewish tradition has required the performance of berit mila specifically on the eighth day even if that day falls on Shabbat.

Circumcision may be postponed for medical reasons. If postponed, it should be held as soon as possible consistent with the health of the child.

Weddings and wedding preparations

Weddings should not take place on Shabbat. In making unavoidable final preparations for a Saturday evening wedding, care should be taken to preserve the spirit of Shabbat.

Mourning on Shabbat

Although Shabbat is counted as one of the days of *shiva* (the first seven days of mourning), mourners do modify their mourning insofar as it is appropriate to observe Shabbat during shiva and to leave the house in order to attend synagogue services.

Funerals are not conducted on Shabbat, nor on the first day or last day of major festivals, since no work may be performed, and the mood of the funeral is contrary to the spirit of rejoicing (oneg) which characterizes Shabbat and the festivals.

Maintaining the special quality of Shabbat

One should maintain and enjoy the special quality of Shabbat throughout the entire day from the lighting of Shabbat candles until the recitation of Havdalah. This may be done by choosing activities to complement and enrich one's spiritual life. Special care should be taken to conduct oneself in such a manner and to participate in such activities as will promote the distinctive Shabbat qualities of kedusha/holiness, menucha/rest, and oneg/joy.

The mitzvah of Havdalah

At the conclusion of Shabbat, it is a mitzvah to recite Havdalah—separating the holy from the ordinary, Shabbat from the other days of the week.

In Conclusion

More than Israel has kept Shabbat, Shabbat has kept Israel.
Ahad Haam, 19th century

This book began with an invitation to explore a variety of ways for making Shabbat a part of your life.

At this point in your reading, you can probably sense how beneficial your embracing Shabbat as described in this guide could be for the Jewish people. As Ahad Haam put it, to the extent that "Israel keeps Shabbat," the Jewish community does become stronger. The more we connect as a group to Judaism in general, and Shabbat in particular, the more vibrant our community can be.

At the same time, Shabbat is not something a Jew observes only because it benefits others. Shabbat is something a Jew can celebrate because it does so much on a personal level for the Jew who takes it seriously.

Especially for Jews in search of ways to express themselves Jewishly, Shabbat provides a marvelous opportunity. It allows those who follow it to give real substance to their individual identity as Jews.

When you observe Shabbat, you are able to go beyond merely talking about Judaism in theory. You encounter it in reality. You literally drink the wine, smell the spices, and study the Torah portion of the week. By observing Shabbat, you experience what the words shalom/peace, menucha/rest, and kedusha/holiness mean. Once a week you allow yourself to come in contact with the actual practices and values that have distinguished Jewish life for centuries. On the seventh day, you truly feel Jewish because Shabbat is the great day of the week set aside for Jewish identification and affirmation.

The irony is that if this guide succeeds in providing an entry point into Shabbat, it may also accomplish something else. Because Shabbat can open the gate to an altogether fuller Jewish life, this guide may prepare you to go beyond Shabbat and into the practices and values of Judaism that obtain every day of the year.

Finding Shabbat can help you ground yourself more intensely and positively as a Jew. It can help you understand this phrase from the prayerbook, that resonates with the joy Jews have always felt about Shabbat and Judaism—

אַשְׁרֵינוּ! מַה טוֹב חֶלְקֵנוּ, וּמַה נָּעִים גּוֹרָלֵנוּ, וּמַה יָּפָה יְרֻשָּׁתֵנוּ!

How happy we are! How good is our portion, how pleasant our lot, how beautiful our heritage!

Further Reading

As your interest in Shabbat grows, you may find some of the following books helpful. In the spirit of exploration that characterizes the rest of this guide, these books represent a wide spectrum of approaches toward Shabbat.

Reform Judaism

Gates of Prayer
Central Conference of American Rabbis, 1975.
> The prayerbook of the Reform movement for daily, Shabbat, and festival use.

Gates of the House: The Union Home Prayerbook
Central Conference of American Rabbis, 1977.
> Prayers for Shabbat along with prayers and an anthology of poetry for other occasions in the Jewish home.

The Jewish Home: A Guide for Jewish Living
Daniel B. Syme, Union of American Hebrew Congregations, 1989.
> A question-and-answer book on Shabbat, the holidays, and the Jewish life cycle.

Liberal Judaism
Eugene Borowitz, Union of American Hebrew Congregations, 1984.
> Reform Jewish belief in a variety of areas, from the observance of ritual to the belief in God.

Liberal Judaism at Home: The Practices of Modern Reform Judaism
Morrison David Bial, Union of American Hebrew Congregations, 1971.
> An overview of Jewish observance.

Shaarei Mitzvah / Gates of Mitzvah: A Guide to the Jewish Life Cycle
Central Conference of American Rabbis, 1979.
> A presentation of the Jewish life cycle with emphasis on the observance of mitzvot.

Shaarei Mo-eid / Gates of the Seasons: A Guide to the Jewish Year
Central Conference of American Rabbis, 1983.
> A presentation of the holiday cycle with emphasis on the observance of mitzvot.

Shaarei Shira / Gates of Song
Transcontinental Music Publications, 1987.
> Musical settings for the texts of *Gates of Prayer*.

A Shabbat Manual
Central Conference of American Rabbis, 1972.
> The first formal guide to Shabbat produced by the Reform rabbinate on this continent.

History and Thought

The Jewish Festivals
Hayyim Schauss, Schocken Books, 1962.
> Shabbat and the other holidays in terms of their historic development.

The Jewish Way: Living the Holidays
Irving Greenberg, Summit Books, 1988.
> A thematic approach to the yearly cycle of the Jewish holidays.

The Sabbath: Its Meaning for Modern Man
Abraham Joshua Heschel, Noonday, 1975.
> A spiritual interpretation of Shabbat for the modern world.

Shabbat Shalom: A Renewed Encounter with the Sabbath
Pinchas H. Peli, Bnai Brith, 1989.
> A collection of short inspirational essays on Shabbat based on ancient and modern sources.

How-to Books and Other Approaches

Come, Let Us Welcome Shabbat
Union of American Hebrew Congregations, 1989.
> An introduction to the Friday night Shabbat experience.

A Guide to Jewish Religious Practice
Isaac Klein, The Jewish Theological Seminary of America, New York, 1979.
> A comprehensive presentation on Jewish practice from the perspective of Conservative Judaism.

How to Run a Traditional Jewish Household
Blu Greenberg, Simon and Schuster, 1984.
> The author shares her enthusiasm for Shabbat, and Jewish living in general, in a modern Orthodox setting.

The Jewish Catalog, Volume 1
Richard Siegel, Michael Strassfeld, Sharon Strassfeld, Jewish Publication Society, 1973.
> One of the first "hands-on" books to explore all aspects of Jewish living; includes excellent material on Shabbat in practice and theory.

Shabbat at Home
Union of American Hebrew Congregations, 1988.
> A small pamphlet with ideas for enhancing the experience at the Erev Shabbat table.

The Shabbat Catalog
Ruth Brin, Ktav Publishing House, 1978.
> Readings, stories, recipes, and more are presented for adults and children.

The Shabbat Seder
Ron Wolfson, Federation of Jewish Men's Clubs, 1986.
> A beautifully conceived guide to the meaning and joy of the Friday evening Shabbat experience in a Conservative context.

To Be a Jew: A Guide to Jewish Observance in Contemporary Life
Hayim Halevy Donin, Basic Books, 1972.
> A very accessible overview of Jewish observance, including Shabbat, in Orthodoxy.

For Children

Come, Let Us Welcome Shabbat
Judyth Saypol and Madeline Wikler, Kar-Ben Copies, 1987.
> Shabbat at home for pre-schoolers.

The Jewish Family Game Book for the Sabbath and Festivals
Ron Isaacs, Ktav Publishing House, 1989.
> Fifty-seven games adapted for the Jewish holiday cycle to be used by families throughout the year.

Shabbat Can Be
Raymond E. Zwerin and Audrey Friedman Marcus, Union of American Hebrew Congregations, 1979.
> A beautiful picture book for pre-schoolers portraying the spirit of Shabbat.

Shabbat Delight: A Celebration with Stories, Games, and Songs
Ron Isaacs, The American Jewish Committee and Ktav Publishing House, 1987.
> For families with young children.

Musical Settings for Prayers and Zemirot/Songs

Along with prayer, study and leisure, music offers a beautiful way to experience the oneg/joy of Shabbat. In the following pages, you will find musical settings for the liturgy plus a selection of zemirot/songs that can be sung at the Shabbat meals or at any other time when people gather together on Shabbat.

You can purchase an audiotape containing the music in this section from Transcontinental Music Publications, Inc., 838 Fifth Avenue, New York, NY 10021. Sheet music with piano arrangements and/or guitar chording for most of these selections is also available from Transcontinental.

Hadlakat Neirot/Candlelighting

Music by A.W. Binder

Serenely

Ba - ruch a - ta A - do - nai, E - lo -
hei - nu me - lech ha - o - lam,_____ a -
sher ki - de - sha - nu be - mits - vo - tav,_____ ve - tsi -
va - nu le - had - lik_____ neir, le - had - lik_____
neir shel Sha - bat.

Shalom Aleichem

Music by I. Goldfarb

Gently

1. Sha - lom a - lei - chem, mal - a - chei ha - sha - reit,
4. Tzeit' - chem le - sha - lom mal - a - chei ha - sha - lom,

mal - a - chei El - yon,_____ mi - me - lech
mal - a - chei El - yon,_____ mi - me - lech

ma - le - chei ham' - la - chim, ha - ka - dosh ba - ruch_____ Hu.
ma - le - chei ham' - la - chim, ha - ka - dosh ba - ruch_____ Hu.

2. Bo - a - chem le - sha - lom, mal - a - chei ha - sha - lom, mal - a - chei El -
chu - ni le - sha - lom, mal - a - chei ha - sha - lom, mal - a - chei El -

yon, mi - me - lech ma - le - chei ham' - la - chim, ha -
yon, mi - me - lech ma - le - chei ham' - la - chim, ha -

ka - dosh ba - ruch Hu.
ka - dosh ba - ruch 3. Bar' - Hu.

Kiddush for Erev Shabbat

Music by L. Lewandowski

Ba - ruch a - ta A - do - nai, E - lo - hei - nu me - lech ha - o -

lam, bo - rei pe - ri ha - ga - fen.

Ba - ruch a - ta A - do - nai, E - lo - hei - nu me - lech ha - o -

lam, a - sher kid' - sha - nu be - mits - vo - tav ve - ra - tsa

va - nu, ve - sha - bat kod - sho be - a - ha - va uv' - ra - tson hin - chi -

la - nu, zi - ka - ron le - ma - a - sei ve - rei - shit. Ki hu yom te - chi - la, le -

mik - ra - ei ko - desh, zei - cher li - tsi - at Mits - ra -

yim. Ki va - nu va - char - ta, ve - o - ta - nu ki -

dash - ta mi - kol ha - a - mim, ve - sha - bat_____

kod - she - cha be - a - ha - va uv' - ra - tson hin - chal - ta -

nu. Ba - ruch a - ta A - do - nai, me - ka - deish ha - sha - bat.

Motsi

Music by S. Adler

Gently moving

Ba - ruch a - ta A - do - nai E - lo - hei - nu me - lech ha - o -

lam, ha - mo - tsi le - chem min___ ha - a - rets.

Shir Hama-alot

Psalm 126

Folksong

Joyfully

Shir___ ha - ma - a - lot. Be - shuv___ A - do - nai___
Shu - va A - do - nai___ et___ she - vi - tei - nu

ct shi - vat Tsi - yon, ha - yi - nu ke - chol - mim.___ Az___ yi - ma - lei se -
ka - a - fi - kim___ ba - ne - gev. Ha - zor - im be -

chok——— pi-nu, ul'-sho-nei-nu ri— na. Az— yom-ru
dim - a, be-ri - na— yik-tso-ru. Ha-loch yei-leich

va - go-yim:"Hig-dil A-do-nai— la-a-sot im ei-leh." Hig-dil A-do-nai
u - va-cho,— no-sei me-shech ha - za-ra, bo-ya-vo

la-a-sot i-ma-nu, ha - yi - nu se-mei - chim!
ve-ri-na,— no - sei— a - lu-mo-tav.

Birkat Hamazon

Traditional

Leader

Cha - vei - rai ne - va - reich!

All, then repeated by Leader

Ye -hi-sheim A-do-nai me-vo-rach mei-a-ta ve-ad o-lam!

Leader

Bir' - shut cha-vei-rai ne-va-reich (E-lo-hei-nu) she-a-chal-nu mi-she-lo.

All, then repeated by Leader

Ba - ruch (E- lo-hei-nu) she - a-chal-numi-she-lo— uv'-tu-vocha-yi - nu.

Leader

Ba - ruch hu, u - va - ruch she - mo!

All

Ba - ruch a - ta— A - do - nai, E - lo - hei - nu me - lech ha - o -

lam, ha - zan et ha - o - lam ku - lo be-tu-vo. Be - chein— be-che-sed uv'-

ra-cha-mim hu no-tein le - chem le-chol ba-sar, ki le - o - lam chas-

do. Uv'- tu - vo ha-ga-dol ta - mid lo cha-sar la-nu,

ve- al yech-sar la-nu ma - zon le-o- lam va - ed, ba - a - vur she-mo ha-ga-

dol.— Ki hu Eil zan um'-far-neis la - kol u - mei - tiv la - kol u-mei-

chin ma - zon le - chol b'ri-yo-tav a - sher—ba - ra. Ba - ruch a - ta, — A - do-

nai, ha - zan et ha - kol. Ka - ka - tuv:

"v'a - chal - ta v'sa - va - ta, u - vei - rach - ta et A - do-

Freely

nai E - lo - he - cha— al ha - a - rets ha - to - va a - sher na - tan lach."

A tempo

Ba - ruch a - ta, A - do - nai,— al ha - a - rets— ve -

al ha - ma - zon. U - ve - nei Ye - ru - sha - la - yim ir ha-

ko-desh bim'-hei-ra ve-ya-mei-nu.____ Ba-ruch a-ta, A-do-

nai,____ bo__ neh ve-ra-cha-mav Ye-ru-sha-la-yim. A-

mein. Ha-ra-cha-man,____ hu yan-chi-lei-nu yom she-ku-

lo Sha-bat u'me nu cha__ le-cha-yei ha-o-la-mim.

O-seh sha-lom bim'-ro-mav, hu ya-a-seh sha-lom a-

lei-nu ve-al kol Yis-ra-eil, ve-i-me-ru: A-mein. A-do-

nai oz le-a-mo yi-tein, A-do-

nai ye-va-reich et a-mo__ va-sha-lom.

Havdalah Blessings

Traditional

Wine / Spices / Light } Ba -ruch a-ta A-do-nai, E- lo -hei- nu me-lech ha-o- lam, { bo- / bo- / bo-

rei___ pe - ri ha - ga - fen.
rei___ mi - nei___ ve - sa - mim.
rei___ me-o-rei___ ha - eish.

Havdalah: Blessing of Separation

Traditional

Ba - ruch a-ta A-do-nai, E- lo -hei- nu me-lech ha-o- lam, ha-mav-

dil bein ko-desh le-chol, bein or___ le - cho-shech, bein Yis-ra - eil la - a-mim, bein

yom hash'- vi - i___ le-shei-shet ye- mei ha - ma - a - seh. Ba -

ruch a- ta, A-do-nai, ha-mav -dil___ bein ko-desh___ le - chol. ___

Hamavdil & Shavu-a Tov

Folksong

Stately

Ha-mav – dil bein ko-desh— bein ko-desh le-chol,

cha-to-tei – nu hu yim-chol, zar-ei-nu ve-chas-pei-nu yar-

Upbeat

beh ka-chol, ve-cha-ko-cha-vim ba-lai-la.— Sha-vu-a tov, sha-

vu-a tov, sha-vu-a tov, sha-vu-a tov, sha-vu-a tov, sha-

vu – a tov, sha-vu-a tov, sha-vu-a tov.

Eiliyahu Hanavi

Folksong

Sweetly

Ei - li - ya - hu ha - na - vi, Ei - li - ya - hu ha - tish - bi;

Ei - li - ya - hu, Ei - li - ya - hu, Ei - li - ya - hu ha - gil - a - di. *Fine*

Bim' - hei - ra ve - ya - mei - nu, ya - vo ei - lei - nu;

D.C. al Fine

im ma - shi - ach ben Da - vid, im ma - shi - ach ben Da - vid.

Al Shelosha Devarim

Pirkei Avot

Music by Ch. Zur

The world depends on three things: on Torah, on worship, and on loving deeds.

Am Yisra-eil Chai

Music by S. Carlebach

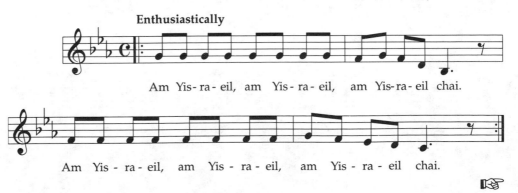

Od A - vi - nu chai, od A - vi - nu chai,

od A - vi - nu, od A - vi - nu, od A - vi - nu chai.

The people of Israel lives. Our God still lives.

Bim Bam

Music by N. Frankel

Cheerfully

Bim bam bim bim bim bam, bim bim bim bim bim

bam. Sha - bat sha - lom Sha - bat sha - lom,

Sha - bat Sha - bat Sha - bat Sha - bat sha - lom. Sha - bat Sha - bat

Sha - bat Sha - bat sha - lom, Sha - bat Sha - bat Sha - bat Sha - bat sha - lom.

Eili, Eili/O God, My God

Lyrics by H. Senesh

Music by D. Zahavi

Ei - li, Ei - li she - lo yi - ga - meir le - o -
lam ha - chol ve - ha - yam rish - rush shel ha -
ma - yim be - rak ha - sha - ma - yim te - fi - lat ha - a -
dam; ha - chol ve - ha - yam rish - rush shel ha -
ma - yim, be - rak ha - sha - ma - yim t'fi - lat ha - a - dam.

O God, my God, I pray that these things nev - er
end: The sand and the sea, the— rush of the—
wa - ters, the— crash of the— hea - vens, the— prayer of the
heart. The sand and the sea, the— rush of the
wa - ters, the crash of the hea - vens, the pray'r of the heart.

Esa Einai

Psalm 121

Music by S. Carlebach

I lift up my eyes unto the mountains. From where does my help come?
My help comes from Adonai, Maker of heaven and earth.

Haleluhu

Psalm 150

Folksong

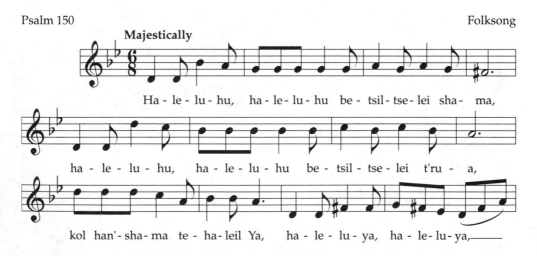

kol han'- sha - ma te - ha - leil Ya, ha - le - lu - ya, ha - le - lu - ya.

Praise God with cymbals sounding; praise God with cymbals resounding.
Let every soul praise God. Halleluyah.

Hinei Ma Tov

Psalm 133

Music by M. Jacobson

Brightly

Hi - nei ma tov u - ma na - im she-vet a-chim gam

1. ya - chad. 2. **Fine** ya - chad. Hi - nei ma tov u - ma na -

im, la, la, la, la, la, la, la, la, la, la.——— Hi -

nei ma tov u - ma na-im, la, la, la, la, la, la, la, la, la, la, hi -

D.C. al Fine

nei ma tov u - ma na-im——— she-vet a-chim— gam— ya-chad.

Behold, how pleasant it is for friends to dwell together.

125

Hinei Ma Tov

Psalm 133

Traditional

Warmly

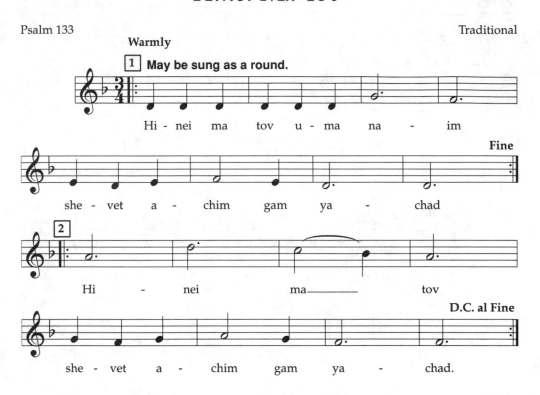

[1] May be sung as a round.

Hi - nei ma tov u - ma na - im

Fine

she - vet a - chim gam ya - chad

[2]

Hi - nei ma_____ tov

D.C. al Fine

she - vet a - chim gam ya - chad.

Ki Eshmera Shabbat

Text by Abraham Ibn Ezra

Baghdad Folksong

Liltingly

Ki esh me- ra Sha - bat Eil__ yish-me - rei - ni,

Fine

ki esh- me- ra Sha - bat Eil__ yish-me - rei - ni.

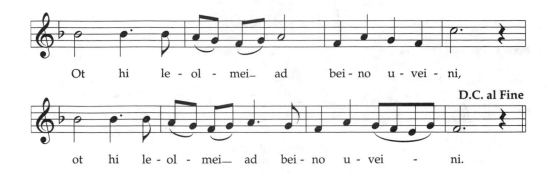

Ot hi le - ol - mei— ad bei - no u - vei - ni,

D.C. al Fine

ot hi le - ol - mei— ad bei - no u - vei - ni.

As I observe Shabbat, God watches over me. It is a sign for ever between God and me.

Lecha Dodi

Text by Solomon Halevi

Music by M. Zeira

Spirited

Le - cha do - di— lik - rat ka - la, lik - rat ka - la,

pe - nei Sha - bat— ne - kab'- la ne - kab'- la. Le - cha do - di lik -

rat ka - la pe - nei Sha - bat ne - ka - be - la. Le -

cha do - di lik - rat ka - la pe - nei Sha - bat ne - ka - be - la.

Come, my beloved, let us go out to meet the bride. Let us greet Shabbat.

Lo Yisa Goi

Book of Isaiah

Folksong

Animated

Lo yi-sa goi el goi che - rev,_____ lo yil - me -

du od mil - cha - ma._____ ma. Lo yi-sa goi el

goi che - rev, lo yil - me - du od— mil - cha - ma, lo yi-sa goi el

D.C. al Fine

goi che - rev, lo yil - me - du od_____ mil - cha - ma.

Nation shall not lift up sword against nation. Neither shall they learn war anymore.

Ma Yafeh Hayom

Folksong

Serenely

Ma ya - feh ha - yom. Sha - bat sha - lom.

Ma ya - feh ha - yom. Sha - bat sha - lom.

Sha - bat Sha - bat— sha - lom, Sha - bat Sha - bat— sha - lom,

Sha - bat Sha - bat— sha - lom, Sha - bat sha - lom.

How beautiful this day is. Shabbat Shalom.

Oseh Shalom

Liturgy

Music by N. Hirsch

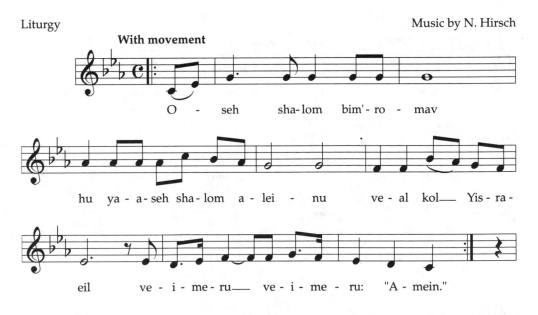

With movement

O - seh sha-lom bim'- ro - mav

hu ya - a - seh shalom a - lei - nu ve - al kol— Yis - ra -

eil ve - i - me - ru— ve - i - me - ru: "A - mein."

Ya - a - seh sha - lom, ya - a - seh sha - lom, sha - lom a - lei - nu ve-

al kol Yis - ra - eil, ya - a - seh sha - lom ya - a - seh sha - lom

sha - lom a - lei - nu ve - al kol Yis - ra - eil. Ya - a - seh sha - lom,

(repeat optional)

ya - a - seh sha - lom, sha - lom a - lei - nu ve - al kol Yis - ra - eil,

ya - a - seh sha - lom ya - a - seh sha - lom sha - lom a - lei - nu ve-

al kol Yis - ra - eil, ya - a - seh sha - lom ya - a - seh sha - lom

sha - lom a - lei - nu ve - al kol Yis - ra - eil.

Sim Shalom

Liturgy

Folksong

Sim sim sim sha-lom___ sim sim sim sha-lom___

sim sim sim sha-lom___ to - va u - ve - ra - cha.

La la la la la la la la la la la la la la la la la

la la la la la la la la la la la la la la.

Grant us peace, goodness, and blessing.

Veshameru

Book of Exodus

Music by M. J. Rothblum

Lively — Refrain

Ve - sha - me - ru ve - nei Yis - ra - eil et ha - sha - bat, la - a - sot et ha - sha - bat le - do - ro - tam be - rit o - lam. lam.

Verse 1

Bei - ni u - vein be - nei Yis - ra - eil ot hi le - o - lam, ot hi le - o - lam. REPEAT REFRAIN

Verse 2

Ki shei - shet ya - mim a - sa A - do - nai et ha - sha - ma - yim ve - et ha - a - rets. REPEAT REFRAIN

Verse 3

U-va- yom ha-she-vi- i, u-va-yom ha-she-vi- i, sha-

D.C. al Fine

vat va-yi - na-fash, sha - vat va-yi - na - fash._____

The people of Israel shall keep Shabbat, observing Shabbat throughout the generations as a covenant for all time. It is a sign for ever between Me and the people of Israel, for in six days God made heaven and earth, and on the seventh day God rested and was refreshed.

Yedid Nefesh

Text by Eliezer Azkari

Music by E. & S. Zweig

Lyrically

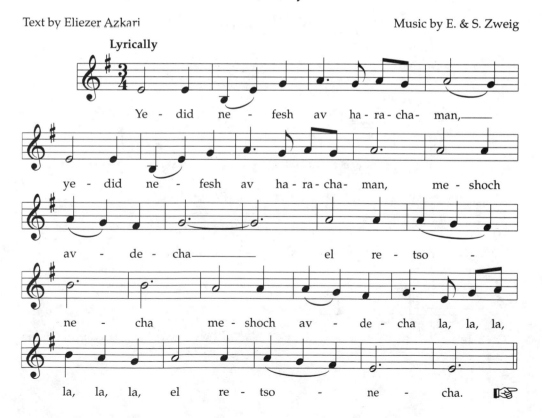

Ye - did ne - fesh av ha-ra-cha- man,_____

ye - did ne - fesh av ha-ra-cha-man, me - shoch

av - de - cha_____ el re - tso -

ne - cha me - shoch av - de - cha la, la, la,

la, la, la, el re - tso - ne - cha. ☞

Ya - ruts____ av - de - cha ke - mo a -

yal,_____ yish - ta - cha - veh la, la, la, la, la, la,

la, la, la, el mul ha - da - re - cha.

Heart's delight, Source of mercy, draw Your servant into Your arms.
I leap like a deer to stand in awe before You.

Yismechu Hashamayim

Psalm 96

Chassidic

Joyfully

Yis - me - chu ha - sha - ma - yim, yis - me - chu ha - sha - ma - yim,

yis - me - chu ha - sha - ma - yim____ ve - ta - geil ha - a - rets.

[1.]

[2.] **Fine**

rets. Yir - am ha - yam, yir - am ha - yam, yir - am ha - yam____ u - me -

loo, lo - o. Yir - am ha-yam, yir - am ha-yam,

yir - am ha - yam— u - me - lo - o, lo - o.—

Let the heavens be glad and the earth rejoice. Let the sea and all within it roar.

Yom Zeh Leyisra-eil

Text by Isaac Luria

Folksong

Lightly

Yom zeh le - yis - ra - eil o - ra ve - sim-cha, o -

ra ve- sim-cha,— Sha - bat me-nu-cha. Yom zeh le - yis - ra - eil o -

ra— ve - sim-cha, Sha - bat— me - nu - cha.

This is Israel's day of light and joy, a Sabbath of rest.

Glossary

Beit Keneset   "House of Assembly." One of three traditional terms describing the functions of the synagogue.

Beit Midrash   "House of Study." One of three traditional terms describing the functions of the synagogue.

Beit Tefila   "House of Prayer." One of three traditional terms describing the functions of the synagogue.

Birkat Hamazon   "The Blessing of Food." The blessing of thankfulness recited after meals.

Challah   Special Shabbat and holiday bread. The name derived from the special dough offering set aside for the priests during the existence of the Temple. After the destruction of the Temple, people continued the practice of setting aside part of the dough when they baked holiday loaves. Eventually the term "challah" was applied to the Shabbat and holiday loaves themselves.

Elijah   Israelite prophet active during the reign of Ahab and Ahaziah (ninth century B.C.E.). According to Jewish folklore, Elijah is the figure destined to announce the coming of the Messiah.

Erev   "Evening, eve." The time prior to the start of Shabbat or a festival. Thus, for example, "Erev Shabbat" refers to Friday, especially the afternoon and early evening before the beginning of Shabbat; "Erev Sukkot" is the day before the first day of Sukkot. In popular parlance, Friday night and the first night of a holiday are often referred to as "Erev Shabbat" or "Erev Sukkot," etc.

Hachnasat Orchim   "Bringing in guests." Home hospitality on Shabbat is a mitzvah.

Hadlakat Neirot   [The mitzvah of] kindling of the candles [on the eve of Shabbat and festivals].

Haftarah	"Conclusion." A section from the prophetic books of the Bible read on Shabbat and holidays after the reading of the Torah.
Halacha	"Law." (From the root meaning "to go," the way in which a Jew should "walk" in life.) Halacha is the term used to describe Judaism's legal tradition.
Havdalah	"Separation." The ceremony marking the end of Shabbat and festivals. The Havdalah blessing separates the holy from the ordinary.
Kabbalat Shabbat	"Welcoming Shabbat." The traditional synagogue service conducted in order to "welcome" the Sabbath bride or queen while the sun sets on Friday evening. The general feeling that Shabbat must be welcomed and prepared for appropriately derives from the image of Shabbat as a day with a personality and holiness of its own. Kabbalat Shabbat can also refer to the welcoming of Shabbat around the dinner table.
Kedusha	"Holiness." The Hebrew word also has the connotation of separation, setting aside.
Kiddush	"Sanctification." Prayers recited, usually over wine, to mark the holiness of Shabbat or festivals. The word is also used as a general term for the festive gathering after a morning service on such days.
Lechem Mishneh	"Two loaves." The two traditional loaves set out in the ancient Temple during Shabbat and festivals.
Maimonides	Rabbi Moses ben Maimon (1135–1204), also known by the acronym Rambam. The foremost Jewish thinker and rabbinic authority of the Middle Ages. His writings include the *Guide of the Perplexed*, the *Mishneh Torah*, and *Sefer Hamitzvot*.
Mechilta	"Measure" or "rule." A collection of *midrash halacha* (see below) based on the Book of Exodus. The Mechilta was compiled in the fourth or fifth century C.E.
Melaveh Malka	"Accompanying/Escorting the Queen." The name given to the meal organized in some communities, particularly Chasidic, that takes place after Havdalah honoring the departure of the Sabbath Queen.

Melacha	"Work." The Talmud enumerates thirty-nine categories of work prohibited on Shabbat.
Menucha	"Rest." The goal of Shabbat achieved by both the abstinence from weekday activities and the pursuit of other activities that "refresh" the soul of the Jew.
Midrash	The method of interpreting scripture to elucidate legal points (*midrash halacha*) or bring out lessons through stories or sermons (*midrash agada*). "Midrash" is also the designation of a particular genre of rabbinic literature extending from pre-mishnaic times to the tenth century. Taken together, the body of works known as Midrash constitutes an anthology of both biblical exegesis and sermonic material.
Mishnah	The first codification of basic Jewish law, arranged by Rabbi Judah Hanasi about 200 C.E. The Mishnah is the nucleus for all halacha. The Mishnah is divided into six major areas of law, each of which is called an order. Each order is further subdivided into subject areas called tractates that deal with specific topics such as Shabbat, marriage, and the ancient Jewish court system.
Mishneh Torah	An encyclopedic legal code in fourteen volumes, also called *Yad Hachazakah*, by Maimonides (see above). The Mishneh Torah covers all halachic subjects discussed in the Talmud and gives clear rulings where there are conflicting opinions.
Mitzvah (Mitzvot)	"Commandment(s)." Religious duty or obligation.
Motsi	"[The one Who] brings forth [bread]." The blessing recited over bread and before eating.
Neshama Yeteira	"An additional soul." According to rabbinic legend, an additional soul dwells in the Jew during Shabbat.
Netilat Yadayim	Literally "lifting up hands." The phrase is used to identify the custom of washing the hands before eating.
Oneg	"Joy, delight." Shabbat is a day of oneg. The term also refers to the social gathering after a Shabbat evening service or to a study session and get-together on Shabbat afternoon.

(The) Rabbis	"My master(s)." The title used to describe the generations of Jewish scholar-leaders who created post-biblical literature such as the Mishnah, Talmud, and various Midrashic texts. The term "sages" is often used interchangeably to describe these same leaders.
Se-uda Shelishit	"The Third Meal." The third of the three meals eaten in honor of Shabbat. Se-uda Shelishit is a light meal eaten toward the end of Saturday afternoon.
Shabbat	"The Sabbath." An occasion for rest and spiritual refreshment, abstention from the concerns of the workaday world, and participation in home and synagogue religious observances.
Shamor	"Observe." In Deuteronomy 5:12 we are commanded, *"Shamor et yom hashabat lekadesho"* ("Observe the Sabbath day to keep it holy").
"Shavu-a Tov!"	"Have a good week!" A greeting at the end of the Havdalah service at the conclusion of Shabbat.
Shulchan Aruch	"A Prepared Table." This four-volume work by Joseph Caro (1488–1575) is the basis for Jewish law today. The Shulchan Aruch codified Sephardic custom. Moses Isserles (1530–1572) supplemented this work with a commentary called Mappah ("Tablecloth"), codifying Ashkenazic custom.
Siddur	"Arrangement." Prayerbook.
Simcha	"Joy, happiness, festivity, joyful occasion."
Talmud	"Study" or "learning." The commentary and discussions of the early rabbis on the Mishnah of Rabbi Judah Hanasi. Divided into the same orders and tractates as the Mishnah, the talmudic discussions are always printed together with their corresponding parts of Mishnah. The Babylonian Talmud is the interpretation and elaboration of Mishnah as developed in the great academies of Babylonia between the third and the fifth centuries, C.E., and is considered more authoritative than the smaller Jerusalem Talmud, developed in the great academies of Palestine before the fifth century.
Talmud Torah	"The study of Torah." The mitzvah of Jewish study.

Tzedakah	"Righteous act; charity." A gift given as an act of justice.
Yom Shekulo Shabbat	"A day of eternal Shabbat." One of the traditional descriptions of the messianic era.
Zachor	"Remember." In Exodus 20:8 we are commanded, *"Zachor et yom hashabat lekadesho"* ("Remember the Sabbath day to keep it holy").
"Zeicher Litsi-at Mitsrayim."	"Memorial to the Exodus from Egypt." A phrase from the Shabbat evening Kiddush. It is based on chapter 5 of Deuteronomy, where Shabbat is referred to as a reminder of the Exodus from Egypt.
Zemirot	"Songs." Special musical selections sung at the table on Shabbat and festivals.

Notes and Acknowledgments

1. Shulchan Aruch, *Orach Chayim* 263:2, 271:2
2. Mechilta *Bachodesh* 7 to Exodus 20:8
3. Talmud *Shabbat* 119a
4. Talmud *Shabbat* 119a
5. Mishnah *Shabbat* 2:1
6. Talmud *Shabbat* 119a
7. Mechilta *Bachodesh* 7 to Exodus 20:8; Talmud *Pesachim* 106a
8. Talmud *Pesachim* 106a
9. Talmud *Avoda Zara* 29b
10. Talmud *Ketubot* 8b
11. Talmud *Yoma* 75b
12. Talmud *Beitsa* 16a
13. Talmud *Shabbat* 113b
14. Mishnah *Berachot* 7:3
15. Pirkei Avot 5:25
16. Talmud *Shabbat* 127a
17. Talmud *Pesachim* 101a
18. Mishnah *Megila* 3:4–6
19. Talmud *Megila* 29b
20. Talmud *Pesachim* 106a
21. The prohibition against kindling a flame, Exodus 35:3. Plowing, harvesting, reaping, Exodus 34:21. Gathering wood, Numbers 15:32–35. Baking and cooking, according to the traditional interpretation, Exodus 16:22. Carrying, Jeremiah 17:21–22, Nehemiah 13:19. Buying and selling, Nehemiah 13:15–17.
22. Talmud *Shabbat* 49b; Mechilta *Shabbata* 2 to Exodus 35:1
23. Mishnah *Chagiga* 1:8
24. Mishnah *Berachot* 8:5
25. Mishneh Torah *Hilchot Shabbat* 29.9
26. Talmud *Shabbat* 35b
27. Tosafot to Talmud *Beitsa* 33b
28. Talmud *Pesachim* 54a
29. Genesis Rabbah 12:5, Talmud *Pesachim* 53b
30. Talmud *Pesachim* 103b
31. Talmud *Ketubot* 62b
32. Genesis Rabbah 17:5, 44:17, Talmud *Berachot* 57b
33. Talmud *Shabbat* 127a, Mishnah *Pei-a* 1:1

Acknowledgments

Every effort has been made to ascertain the owners of copyrights for the selections used in this text and to obtain permission to reprint copyrighted passages. For the use of the passages indicated, the Central Conference of American Rabbis expresses its gratitude to those whose names appear below. The Conference will be pleased, in subsequent editions, to correct any inadvertent errors or omissions that may be pointed out.

ACUM HOUSE. ISRAEL: "Hinnei Mah Tov," Copyright by Moshe Jacobsen. Reprinted by permission of Acum House.

ACUM HOUSE. ISRAEL: "Oseh Shalom," Copyright by Nurith Hirsch. Reprinted by permission of Acum House.

FALK, MARCIA: "Light a Candle" by Zelda, translated from the Hebrew by Marcia Falk, copyright 1991 by Marcia Falk. Used by permission of the translator.

HARCOURT BRACE JOVANOVICH INC: Excerpt from "The Conduct of Life," Copyright 1951 and renewed by Lewis Mumford in 1975. Reprinted by permission of Harcourt Brace Jovanovich.

HARVARD UNIVERSITY PRESS: "Meditation and Sabbath," by Harvey Cox. Copyright 1977. Reprinted with permission by *Harvard Magazine*.

HENRY HOLT & COMPANY, INC: From "You Shall Be As Gods," by Erich Fromm. Copyright 1966 by Erich Fromm. Reprinted by permission of Henry Holt and Company Inc.

Judaism, VOLUME 32, NUMBER 1 (WINTER 1983) p. 56; poem by Tzvi Yair is reprinted by permission of the American Jewish Congress.

Judaism, VOLUME 31, NUMBER 1 (WINTER, 1982) p. 10; passage by Robert Gordis is reprinted by permission of the American Jewish Congress.

MIFALEI TARBUTH V'CINUCH. ISRAEL: "Eili, Eili," Copyright for lyrics by Hana Senesh, for music by David Zehavi. Reprinted by permission of Acum House.

MIFALEI TARBUTH V'CINUCH. ISRAEL: "L'cha Dodi," Copyright by Mordechai Zeira. Reprinted by permission of Acum House.

OR-TAV PUBLISHING. ISRAEL: "Al Sh'loshah D'varim," Copyright by Chaim Zur. Reprinted by permission of Acum House.

OR-TAV PUBLISHING. ISRAEL: "Y'did Nefesh," Copyright by E. & S. Zveig. Reprinted by permission of Acum House.

PRAYERBOOK PRESS: For use of several passages in "Likrat Shabbat." Copyright by Prayerbook Press, a subsidiary of Media Judaica Inc.

RECONSTRUCTIONIST PRESS: From the passage, "Accept our gratitude...." Copyright by Ruth Firestone Brin in 1986, in *Harvest: Collected Poems and Prayers*.

RECONSTRUCTIONIST PRESS: From the passage, "Lord, help us now to make this new Shabbat." Copyright by Ruth Firestone Brin in 1986, in *Harvest: Collected Poems and Prayers*.

RECONSTRUCTIONIST PRESS: From the passage, "An Artist Cannot Be...." by Mordecai Kaplan in *The Meaning of God in Modern Jewish Religion*. Copyright by the Reconstructionist Press and used by permission of the Reconstructionist Press.

Reform Judaism (FALL 1983): From a passage on "The Work That is Forbidden," by Arnold Jacob Wolf. Reprinted by permission of the author.

TOWNHOUSE PRESS: From the passage, "Glory Be to You for Chance Encounters...." by Danny Siegal, in *The Lord is a Whisper at Midnight*. Copyright 1985 by the Town House Press and reprinted with their permission.

TOWNHOUSE PRESS: From the passage, "Erev Shabbat...it's so stupid...," by Danny Siegal, in *Nine Entered Paradise Alive*. Copyright 1985 by the Town House Press and reprinted with their permission.

UNION OF AMERICAN HEBREW CONGREGATIONS: From the passage, "Shabbat Can be Different" in *Shabbat Can Be*.

Index